Romancing My Fantasies

Teri Galea-Thorne

Revelations of a heartbroken soul

Published in Australia by Sid Harta Books & Print Pty Ltd,
ABN: 34632585293
23 Stirling Crescent, Glen Waverley, Victoria 3150 Australia
Telephone: +61 3 9560 9920, Facsimile: +61 3 9545 1742
E-mail: author@sidharta.com.au

First published in Australia 2022
This edition published 2022
Copyright © Teri Galea-Thorne 2022
Cover design, typesetting: WorkingType (www.workingtype.com.au)

The right of Teri Galea-Thorne to be identified as the Author of the Work
has been asserted in accordance with the Copyright, Designs and Patents Act 1988.

All rights reserved. No part of this publication may be reproduced,
stored in a retrieval system, or transmitted, in any form or by any means without the prior
written permission of the publisher, nor be otherwise circulated in any form of binding or
cover other than that in which it is published and without a similar condition being imposed
on the subsequent purchaser.

Teri Galea-Thorne
Romancing My Fantasies
ISBN: 978-0-6484916-7-5
pp180

ABOUT THE AUTHOR

Teri Galea-Thorne was born in Sydney, Australia, but raised in Townsville, North Queensland. She graduated from James Cook University in 1999 with a Bachelor of Arts, majoring in English. Teri has worked in various industries, notably insurance, and currently works in a warehouse distributing bread products. Her experiences  have granted her a point of view on life she believes most would not know or understand. Writing has always been her muse and solace, although until now she has never been published. Most of her more than twenty manuscripts are science-fiction / fantasy. In 2014, she undertook a course in scriptwriting and has had a few plays produced in Townsville since 2015, including three major productions. A recent play was accepted in a workshopping competition. She still lives in Townsville with her mother and Cardigan Welsh corgi, Princess.

INTRODUCTION

How often do you reminisce about your past? How much does it influence your future? How much do you regret? Could life have been different? Do you ever wonder?

I wonder how my life would have been if I had 'done that', or 'ventured there', or if 'that would have worked out' or if I chose a path other than my whimsical 'let's see where it takes me' route. When I see other people's lives appearing to be better than mine, I wonder where mine went wrong. Is it jealousy? Possibly.

This book was started as the result of two dreams: one with a helicopter accident and trying to survive it, and about six days later, another dream with the face of a celebrity whom I have not thought about for nearly twenty-five years.

And silly me looked him up on the internet to see what he's been up to. Big mistake. It brought back feelings I had long since buried.

I know sometimes thinking of the past can hold you back, but in another way, it's like therapy and can liberate you. It's not about pondering what life could have been like if you did different things, it's about understanding why you face the problems you do and accepting the fact you made mistakes. And in the end, it is the choices you have made for yourself. You cannot blame anyone else, unless of course they forced you against your will.

My past is not a mistake. There are many things I could have done differently and, yes, there were blunders. But I grew from them and learnt my lessons. However, today I find myself seeking something else other than what I have and, looking back, I tried desperately to find it. What I found is that my experiences have put me into a place I am not sure I can escape. I fear meeting people; I fear letting them in and I keep them at a distance; I fear entering a relationship; and I am unable to make a decent friend. The reasons for these will be explained by what I am about to reveal.

Let me state this: I'm not crazy. I'm sure if any psychologist sat me down they would discover I am very well adjusted and grounded. I think I should have a certificate stating, 'Certifiably Sane'. Hell, I should get a bravery award for simply writing this book. To share with the whole world some of the things within these pages, intimate things, is scary. Will you look at me with some weird idea that I'm a nut? It's not what I'm aiming for, but it could happen. (*I like walnuts by the way*). This is my story, my intimate story. A better analogy would be a celebrity's sex tape — although I think theirs would be far spicier than mine. I will share with you encounters of love, fantasy, romance and sex, and show how I came to be who I am, what I am, and how I perceive everything and everyone around me.

I know not all people are bad, but the majority of people I met have done something to drive back my confidence, my courage, my desire that, if someone nice comes along, I won't have it in me to let them in. Simply put, I don't trust people. 'Why?' you might ask.

All I can say is, we all make mistakes. It is from those mistakes we learn and grow, advancing our intelligence and becoming the person we see every day in the mirror. (*My god, where did that wrinkle come from?*)

A word of warning, my opinions might offend people. It isn't my intention. But I have a right to voice my opinions — everyone else does. They are the essence of me, formed from my observations and experiences. They are not meant to cause harm. If they do, perhaps you should look inside yourself to find out why. I cannot answer the question for you. I am merely warning you: read this book with caution. Try to keep an open mind. And even perhaps put yourself in my position to try to understand how it felt, how you would feel if it happened to you.

I wanted to make this a comedy. After all the crap I have

experienced, there had to be a joke to it all, somewhere. But the more I wrote, the more depressed I got. (*Amazing how one little piece of internet research could have unleashed all this.*) I was hoping to look at my past and laugh it off. But often I cringed, yelling at myself, 'What the hell were you doing?'

But you can't cry over spilt milk. And I suppose I can laugh at my mistakes now, at least some of them. If you can't laugh at life, what's the point of living it?

My paranoia is dictating, 'don't name names.' After some friendly advice, it was decided to give pseudonyms instead. This writing experience opened my eyes. By revealing names, I could be ruining their reputations or intruding on their privacy. Not my intention. Only want to show how their interaction with me moulded my opinions, beliefs and life.

All the names in this book are fictitious, but the people are real. Using mythological names was interesting, but their meanings have no bearing on who these people are. I used them because I feel these names would not be common or much used at all today. (*If someone does have any of these names, forgive me for using them, but they are not you*). I made every effort to mask any characterisation, to avoid identification. Protecting the guilty perhaps? More importantly, protecting me from their wrath. People are far too sensitive these days and a simple little word can cause nightmares. I've been bullied all my life; I don't need to add to it. And even if I wanted to use their real names, most of them dodge recollection.

All but two people mentioned in this book have no idea

this is being published. I have not discussed anything with them and they will be unaware of this publication. The downside to this is that these people are going to know I am talking about them because I was part of their lives. Please understand, I don't hate you. While you treated me kindly in the beginning of our relationship, the experience in the end helped shape my life and guide my choices. And perhaps you might learn something of yourself from how I perceived you treated me but take it with a grain of salt. And given I have changed your names and removed as much characterisation as possible, you take the risk of identifying yourselves. And as for the celebrities I mention — not by name — I never met these people. They don't even know I exist (*well, they will now*).

As for the two who know this is being published; one wanted an alias, the other didn't care as it was my story. I hope both men accept that in writing what I have written, I believed I was being kind in my choice of words because they were kind to me.

I have also made every effort to not name any organisation in order to avoid some idiot thinking I believed they had something to do with my problems and thereby create a defamation case against me. I am in no way trying to ruin anyone's reputations or destroy their images. This is my love story. The path I was forced into, the direction it took me and how I ended up where I am. I will do with it what I will.

Please take a trip down memory lane with me as I reveal my deepest, darkest secrets; unravel the reasons behind my insistence on keeping people away; the fabric of my opinions' foundation. I will attempt to place these memories in chronological order the best I can, but dates elude me like names. After all, these things happened a long time ago. (*Possibly in another galaxy*).

DEDICATION

I would like to dedicate this book to two people:

First, to my mother, Mary Thorne: I don't know why I didn't approach you when all this was happening to me, but you have been there for me for everything else. You are an angel, my foundation of sanity and the greatest friend anyone could wish to know.

Second, to the artist I fantasied about: You don't know me, but you were there for me when I needed someone the most, albeit a figment of my imagination. You helped stop the suicidal thoughts.

I hope you are happy in everything you do and found joy in life.

CHAPTER 1

Insert dream sequence here

Where to start a book on love, romance and stupid mistakes? Logic dictates from the first person you involved yourself with or when you first fell in love. Does it have to be a real person? Common sense is screaming 'Duh!' But for me, my first love was a fantasy.

It was 1988. It was my first year of high school. I was placed in an all-girls Catholic college because my mother believed if I went to a co-ed school, I'd be raped or get into drugs. I had far more chance of getting assaulted at the college than anywhere else, especially after seeing two girls giving each other hickeys before our religion class started. Seriously, one girl was kissing the other's stomach.

And the amount of bullying was insidious. I'm surprised they never jumped me for the fun of it. As for drugs? I made a friend in one term, and she disappeared the next. They kicked her out because she had about $200 worth of marijuana in her bag. At least, that was the excuse I was given.

To say I am Catholic is a lie. While I was born, baptised and raised a Catholic, one little event at this college swayed my opinion away. And I haven't practiced the faith since. At the start of one religion class, our principal — a kind woman whose habit I believe got in the way this day — greeted us. One sentence from her speech will remain with me for eternity.

'I don't care if you fail math, English or science. You cannot fail religion.'

It felt like she was dictating my path to be solely sold to the church. I couldn't see me as a nun. There was more to life than religion. Henry VIII left the Catholic church because they wouldn't give him a divorce. He founded the Anglican church. Hell, if a king could walk away from the church, why couldn't I?

Don't get me wrong, I don't hate religion. I don't despise anyone who believes it. I respect them. It's their choice. Respect is not only the foundation of all religions, but also the key to good living. But I can't stand it when everyone thinks religion is the be-all and end-all of life in general.

I abhor people expecting you to switch your faith to suit them and they don't care about, or respect, your feelings on the matter, and when you don't change, they leave without any regard for your opinions or free will. Religion is supposed to teach respect, isn't it? Yet many religious people never gave me any. And don't get me started on terrorists.

CHAPTER 1 Insert dream sequence here

There have been three incidents in my life where religious people basically proved to me it is all a bunch of hypocrisy. (*I did warn you about my opinions*). Incident number one was when a family who used to be friends with us, wanted us to change our faith. We didn't and they had nothing more to do with us. Too bad their kids got along well with us and vice versa. Our parents made the decision. The second event occurred with one of my romantic interactions. I will leave this until I discuss them. And the third was with Mars One.

Mars One started in 2011. By 2013 they had recruited 1,058 people from 107 countries. I would have loved to sign up but I am an unqualified person, well, not up to their standards anyway. And while this incident didn't affect me personally, it spelled hypocrisy in one sentence. An imam from Iran was quoted as advising all followers of the Islamic faith in these words:

No one is to apply [to Mars One] because it states in the Koran, taking a path that leads to suicide is a sin.

I looked at that sentence over and over. My mind yelled at me, 'Is he serious?' as another idea popped up, ramming it hard against my internal cranium. 'Can you explain suicide bombers for me?' (*This is a request for knowledge to understand, not a challenge.*)

Everyone has the right to believe what they want. No one has the right to make you believe something you cannot bring yourself to believe in. And no one has the right to force his or her ideas on you. How can you respect someone who tries?

How can you respect someone who doesn't respect you? If you want respect, you must first give it, true, and I do respect religious people. But it seems they don't respect me. Well, those I have met anyway.

When our principal nun said those hurtful words, I lost all respect for the religion. It felt like they didn't care about my future. It felt like they were dictating it. A perfect reason to leave the faith.

Trying to fit in and make friends at that school was harder than winning the lottery. It wasn't without trying, mind you. I did try, very hard. But no matter what I did, I found it didn't work. And yes, I know you can't please everyone, but why do those who don't like you have to make you feel like something that gets scraped off in a gutter?

I was never physically bullied. I think that would have been better than what they did to me. Mental scars are difficult to heal, if ever they do. Obviously, mine still run deep if I can put them down on paper. A part of me wanted them to hit me, to give me evidence of the torture. And lack of physical violence masks the severity of what the mental abuse is doing. No one believes you or tells you to *'suck it up, princess'*. They have no clue about the damage inflicted.

What happened at that school? Bullying galore and no solutions to fix the problem. My parents' advice was to stand up for myself. When I did, I got into trouble with the teachers. They didn't want to hear my explanation. To a hormone-inflicted new teenager, advice that doesn't work is bad advice which translates into, 'Never ask them again'. Solutions did not work. I had to look elsewhere. I could have asked my parents to intervene, but it would most probably have made matters worse, like making the bullies resort to physical violence as well and I'd have double the trouble to deal with, despite saying I wish they did. I could have shifted to another school. Well, I did in the end. It didn't help.

What does a teenager with uncontrollable emotions do when she thinks there are no solutions to her problems and cannot find the right people to help her? She resorts to the most heinous act a human can inflict on themselves.

Suicide.

I tried it, twice. I tried overdosing on paracetamol. Not a good way to go because you get sick first and your system simply cannot take anymore. It also runs the risk of liver failure. Currently, mine is functional.

And drowning isn't as easy as it sounds. You really need someone to help hold your head under water. I used my dad's diving weights around my neck. We had an above-ground pool with a set of plastic ladders, one on the outside to access the pool, and the other on the inside to climb out. The inner ladder was weighed down with something heavy in the base — sand, I believe — keeping them submerged. I lifted this base and laid it on my stomach. This, plus the weights, made trying to reach the surface for air very difficult. I had to use my hands on the steps to climb up the ladder. Not easy with weights tied around your neck.

If the water was deeper, I might have succeeded in exhausting my life. I tried this several times. The last was almost successful. As I breached the surface, I took in a desperate breath. Took in some water too. Think this is how I ended up with bronchitis.

An act like suicide reveals two people inside you; 'Little Miss Lost Hope' and 'Ms Slap the Face and Grow Up'. As nasty as the latter sounds, she is in fact the one who saves your life. She is the essence of your soul who clings to life, who ensures life will always win and you will survive whatever calamity befalls you. However, if you bleed, she has no control over that fate. Your body needs blood to function, and she is simply all soul. It's not like she can stop the blood flowing. She hangs on to dear life until there is nothing left.

Little Miss Lost Hope is the stupid one, a part of your soul that has died and manifested into thoughts of self-harm. She can control the body. She can pick up the knives — and yes, I held a few against my wrists, (*I have a small scar to prove it*). An evil thought once plagued my mind to plunge one through my heart. She can evaluate the situation and how to use it to her advantage to inflict pain and death. But most important of all, she is the part you really wish you never had. She makes terrible mistakes.

My two suicide attempts, lousy and weak as they were, taught her a good lesson, which in turn taught me. The will for life is stronger than the wish for death. And, most importantly, death is not the answer.

CHAPTER 1   *Insert dream sequence here*

What else is there for a bullied person with no support to do? I don't know what others do, but what I did at the time seemed like a good idea. It worked for a while too. Its sinister side didn't manifest itself until much later. I created an imaginary friend. It had no form. It had no shape. It was not designated male or female (*the term non-binary wasn't discovered then*). It simply existed. At first it had no voice. It was merely the boxing bag for my grief. I would talk to it, unleash my frustrations on it and relieve my stress to it.

Sometimes it identified itself as my Raggedy Ann doll. You know the ones, right? What I did to that doll frightens me to this day. I feel sick even thinking about it. My poor little doll suffered being drawn on, holes punched into her, thrown from the second floor to the ground, tied to a fan and switched on to fly off, and stomped on, very heavily. I certainly wasn't a kind master. I was that doll's worst enemy. Thank God I don't do that anymore.

It wasn't a single bullying session that unleashed this fury from me. It was the entire school experience, from one year to the next. No matter what school it was. I do not remember kindergarten, but mum tells me it was where I learnt to shove everything under my bed to clean my room. At kindergarten I was the one designated to clean everyone else's toys. For some reason, at home I refused to do this chore. In my older life, this evolved into laziness. I see things that require moving, but simply don't do it until I need them or when they start annoying me. I don't even make the bed in the morning. Why bother when you'll be in it again later? Bad habits follow you until death do you part. Although I am trying to rectify this problem.

For primary school, years one to four were spent at a Catholic college. Again, mum told me that in Year One, an older male student grabbed my head and slammed it into the side of a bus. Guess the memory was smashed out of me. One day I ventured to the out-of-bounds area with a group of kids, finding a snake's skin (*it was all bushland behind the school in those days*) and, when returning, I never heard the bell and had to ask someone if it had gone. She looked at me like I was stupid and called me as such. There was a boy who offered to show a group of us girls his genitals. There was an area between the classrooms at the back where it was kind of secluded. A few of us went and sure enough, he wiggled it at us. Afterwards he asked to see our private parts. We laughed and said, 'No way,' running off.

In Year Two, a cute boy sat opposite me. He would always look at me and, when I returned his gaze, he quickly dropped his. I think, even at that age, he was smitten. He could have been playing a game for all I know; he was shy and timid. I don't think playing games was his style. He had the sweetest smile. Gorgeous.

One teacher was appalled by my writing. Instead of being supportive or using positive reinforcement, she made me stand at the front of the class and explained very harshly that I needed spaces between my words. To demonstrate, she wrote a word on a page, grabbed my hand and forced my index finger next to the word before writing the next one. It was embarrassing. Year One springs to mind, and I think my fear of teachers came from her. It's why I never stood up against those in secondary college who told me off for defending myself.

I loved my grades two and three teachers though. They were kind and I liked them. There was a male teacher in Year Four who taught us music. He played *American Pie* on the guitar.

There was another boy, a strange boy, who uttered something about when we were older he was going to marry me. Imagine, boys at that age thinking of marriage. I didn't even know what the concept was, despite having parents.

And yes, there is a name I evoke with a bitter taste. She was nasty to me. She made going to school difficult. I believe going to Hell would have been better. Satan would have been nicer. Strange how her name remains but her bullying techniques are gone, but with all the other bullies in my life their influence remains but their names are suppressed. Should it matter? None of them deserve recognition.

The years 1985 and 1986 were spent in Fiji. Dad got a promotion and moved the family there. I did have a great friend, at least I thought she was. Vesta *(remember, fake name)*. She was a very fast runner. And I was very competitive *(still am really)*. We visited one of the islands for a holiday and there was this large mango tree on the hill. We saw a ripe mango and both ran for it. I put in all my effort to beat her. I pushed my legs as fast as I could, believing they would catch fire with friction. I reached the mango first. I grabbed it. I stopped. I paid no attention that within a few more steps I would have been flying over the cliff to jagged rocks below. But at least I got the mango.

Our class would stand out in the courtyard for physical education sessions. They had us standing there with our arms stretched out wide. They kept us there until one by one students sat down because they couldn't hold their arms up anymore. Vesta and I were always the last to sit. We flatly refused to lower our arms before the other, despite how much our muscles begged us to. She was a kind and sweet person. I miss her. Wonder if she remembers me?

Others in my class were horrors. One day a bunch of girls surrounded me intent on teaching me a nasty lesson on how and why what happens in movies cannot happen in real life. I said something about defending myself from many targets. They proved me wrong. No real punches were thrown, but one would grab me and, as I defended myself, someone from behind would do the same thing. It wasn't a pleasant experience. Movies can have bad influences on a child's mind.

In 1987 we returned to Townsville. Mum put me in yet another Catholic college, my last primary school. And the bullying got worse. No matter how many times I told students I was born in Sydney, because I spent two years in Fiji, they kept calling me Fijian. I didn't feel hurt being called a Fijian; I took offence at them not listening to me. Despite their attempts to strip away my identity, as if saying I could no longer call myself Australian, the only thing I could do was ignore them. Some went out of their way to remind me, 'You're Fijian. What is that like?'

We had a parade with our class dressed up in costumes. I had this cardboard boat which I could step into and have straps over my shoulders to hold it. We paraded our costumes around and moved to the side. I had to take the boat off to sit. When the awards came, I stood and put it on again because we had to show the costume one more time before accepting the award. I wasn't anticipating winning but wanted to be ready if I did. Others said, 'Why do you think you're gonna win? It's not that good.' I did win. It didn't score me any friends.

Friends were in such short supply at this school, I had none, despite the fact there were thirty of us in the classroom. Often, at break and lunch, I would find myself around the back of the school to find a shady secluded spot and eat in peace. I would always have a book with me. I was a bookworm because I had no social connections. Books were my friends.

The bullying continued into 1988. My imaginary friend appeared like a gift from Heaven. And I tried to survive the best I could, but it felt with every step forward I was being punched back a dozen more.

What you need to know about imaginary friends is that they morph into whatever your desires need at the time. They don't remain an empty shell forever. They change. And this is where the sinister side emerges.

In 1989, still at the same school (*I stayed till the end of 1991*), a band released a song. As I have not received permission to use their name or the artist in question, I can't say who they are. But there was something about them I found appealing (*as thousands of other girls probably did too*). It could have been a high school crush, a spark of youthful stupidity, or perhaps because I was denied a boyfriend my heart desired one. And when my imaginary friend latched on to the personification of one of them, I was doomed.

Hormones raging, emotions boiling on the surface, no social connections to help me understand what the hell was going on inside my body or to help what was happening outside it, and my mind gave me a real face, a real body, a real person to fantasise about, with no other explanation or reason than, 'Hey, use this guy to help solve your problems.'

He didn't help. He became a new problem (*sorry, mate*). Imaginary friends inflict a bad influence, better known as an obsession. It's their sinister side. And I had it bad.

And why only the one? What was special about him which forced my mind to ensnare him into its mould? Why not the other members of the band? Simple. It was some bad advice my mother gave me. One day, she must have had an argument with dad. He was five years her junior. What she told me, allowed my mind to clasp an iron grip around the artist, welding it shut with no hope of release.

She said, 'If you're ever going to marry someone, always choose older and no more than five years.'

Honestly, I don't think age has much to do with love

— with exception of eighty-year-olds marrying eighteen-year-olds. Still can't wrap my head around that one. But that artist is four years older than me; the others didn't make the cut.

And in that instance my first love was over a guy who didn't even know I existed. He still doesn't. Often kids turn to celebrities for inspiration, guidance and emotional connections, especially when everything else fails. No wonder parents have a hard time. How can they compete with superstars? How can they match a child's imagination and lack of experience? How can a child understand that a figment of their imagination cannot be compared to a real person? The object of obsession could never stack up against such perfection.

Did I fantasise having naked romps with him? I was fourteen with hormones out of control. What do you think? But at least I can be honest to say not all my fantasies with him were of a sexual nature. It's not the only thing my body desired. He came into my life at a time when I needed someone the most. Yes, I know it was not actually him, it was my imagination using his face. (*I hope he doesn't charge me for using his likeness*). But his appearance on the world stage was a blessing because my mind needed something to focus on other than the torture and abuse from bullies. He happened to be the poor victim of my immature youth.

An imaginary friend does not remain in the same form forever. The concept morphs into desires. And I did desire a boyfriend when I created the beast — can't call it a friend really, considering what it did with the man's likeness. Why did it morph into him in the first place?

Well, I can thank my mother for this problem. One rule she applied to me was, 'no boyfriend until you are eighteen'. Too bad she let my sister date guys. I was not a rebellious child to simply do what I wanted and go against my mother's wishes. That was not in me. How could it be? I was bullied relentlessly from kids and teachers alike. To have my mother on my back would have made it a triple whammy. I did not need that. Besides, the bullying environment and how I had to deal with it proved I could not go up against my mother. I didn't have it in me.

But when my sister married in 1992, I was seventeen. At the reception, the bride and groom had not even left for the night when mum came up to me and said, 'I think it's time you had a boyfriend.'

A bit bloody late. I was at a point in my life — yes, from that early age — of keeping to myself and not wanting anything to do with anyone, despite still fantasising about an artist who had no clue I was alive. I was merely trying to survive high school. And it felt like even mum was against me. That one simple little remark had conspiracy plastered all over it, like it was a plan between my mother and sister to ensure I remained single, maybe to avoid competition of boyfriends between my sister and me. Not that it would have mattered. Men fancied her more than me anyway.

One night we went to a restaurant at a hotel for dinner.

CHAPTER 1   *Insert dream sequence here*

There was a construction site nearby busy with tradespeople. When we came back to the car, there was a note on the windshield from one of them hoping to score a date with 'the lady in red'. It wasn't my dress, mine was blue. It was my sister. Men really noticed her more than me anyway. She had the height. All I had was blonde hair.

Jealousy? At that time, yes. But everything that happened around me had the mark 'bullying' all over it, like the entire world wanted to inflict pain on me. It was like I was being punished for a past-life crime, one I had no recollection of committing or even knowing I had a past-life. I could not escape it. This is the result of being bullied. Everything that occurred had this lingering doubt of 'is it sincere or is it harassment?' I questioned and doubted everything. Trust no longer existed in my life.

Having been given the green light to get a boyfriend, how does one approach it? My heart and desire were set on a clueless artist. I was deep within obsession, it would have been a massive red flag for him. And considering everyone was bullying me, making a friend was hard enough, now I had to find a boyfriend. Really? I dared not even try. Bullying marred any ability even to make an attempt.

Had I known the trouble that artist would bring to my life, I would never have invented the imaginary friend in the first place. But we all make mistakes. This was my first — or perhaps fourth. My first mistake was allowing the bullies to continue their assault. My second, not informing my parents.

The third, suicide. And perhaps I can squeeze another one in there with not reporting the teachers. But without mistakes, we cannot grow.

CHAPTER 2

A bullied person has few friends

What was terrible about being bullied if I wasn't punched, kicked, groped or injured physically? At least with physical injuries they can heal and be fixed within a few days or weeks. And you might be left with a scar to show off your wounds, to prove you survived the torture.

Mine were all mental. These injuries are invisible. Their vicious fingers worm their way into your mind, twist it to breaking point, corrupt its thoughts — either against you or against others — and take years to heal, if ever they do.

Mental capacity is what allows the body to function. When your mind is sick, your body suffers. When your mind goes AWOL, your body can commit erroneous mistakes or crimes. When your mind is attacked, you spend what little energy you have left defending it, leaving yourself vulnerable when it is all spent.

Memories of my infant years have most likely been written over by all the other years of living, and my brain has no backups. It felt as if from the very beginning I was bullied. Naturally, I am talking about school and not my baby years. Primary school was merely a warm-up to secondary. And it all started with my name. Should my parents have named me something else? No. It wouldn't have mattered to these girls. They would still have found a way to insult me.

All manner of names were spat at me with spite. 'Bitch' hurt a lot and was the most prominent, despite the saying, 'Sticks and stones may break my bones, but names will never hurt me' ringing in my ears because it was my parents' advice. In short, it was a load of baloney. Names don't simply hurt, they sting. They tie up your identity and whip it relentlessly until it bleeds to oblivion.

The one name that bugged me the most was Teresa Green.

First, my real name is Therese. Second, my last name is Thorne. It isn't even spelt like a thorn on a bush. How my name changed to Green was beyond me. Perhaps I was related to Rachel from *Friends*? Was it conceivable I married a Mr Green somewhere along my thirteen years by some bizarre, arranged marriage I was never made aware of but should have known about? When I corrected them, they ignored the advice. When I told them off, I was the one who got into trouble. I'm glad they didn't hear my uncle call me 'Th — reese' because of the 'h' in my name. It is a silent one by the way, like the 'p' in pneumonia. (*Sanity asks, 'why the hell is it there?*') But at least you can't get 'Trees Are' out of 'Th — reese'. Probably why they never picked on it.

As I could not stand up for myself in a physical or verbally vicious way, I had to find an alternative. I was always good with words, allowing me to create eloquent responses to counter their attacks.

The incorrect name of Teresa Green received, 'Yep, I know they are. Glad you're paying attention in your science class.' And my response to the 'bitch' remark? I smiled and said, 'Thank you.'

One girl snapped back, 'Hey, I just called you bitch.'

I thanked her again, even faking a little blush.

'You're a bitch.'

'Why, thank you.' I would like to think I fluttered my eyelashes at her, but I would have been too scared to do that and suffer the consequences should she react violently.

This kept up for a while before she had to ask why I was thanking her. I could have stayed silent to bug her, give her my own little bullying righteousness. But I had to prove to her how stupid she was, a far better justice. I looked her in the eyes, smiled and answered the following:

Bitch is a female dog.

Dogs bark.

Bark is on trees.

Trees are nature.

Nature is beautiful.

Thank you.

I was never called 'bitch' again.

Yes, I did defend myself in some sense. Like the time someone was glaring at me. I simply met her eyes in a brief second and she snapped at me, with a venomous sting, 'What are you looking at?' as if trying to flay my skin off with her words.

It happened often and I created many responses. None, however, stopped her retorting the remark at me. My three favourites were:
1. 'I don't know, it hasn't been discovered yet.'
2. 'I'm not sure, it doesn't have a tag.'
3. 'I don't know, but I'm sure it cracked the mirror this morning.'

But these responses still did not grant me friends. Tugging at my identity and calling me names were only the tip of the iceberg. There was one time when a girl hit my knuckles with the edge my own ruler while we were in class. I think this was my only physical abuse. I asked her to stop. She didn't. The more I asked, the more she denied the request, hitting harder. Eventually, I grabbed the ruler and broke it in front of her. It was mine anyway, I could do what I wanted. But the teacher lectured me about respecting personal property. She didn't want to hear excuses. Not only did the little witch get satisfaction from hitting me, but she also got pleasure watching me be berated.

In 1989 administration arranged to have the old tuckshop building torn down to erect a new one. They hired a demountable to hold the tuckshop at the back of the school. It was bedlam to get anything because the queue was huge.

I was standing in line. I think I was about fourth from the window and these girls who constantly bullied me approached, dumped all their money in my hands and said, 'You can get me this, you can get me that.' They rattled off a list and walked off to sit under a shady tree. I approached the window, ordered what I wanted and returned to them. I gave them their money and said, 'Get it yourself.' Why should I help them when they never appreciated me?

During one of our swimming sessions at a public pool a group of girls tried to get me to spread my legs in a provocative manner. I refused and they said, 'You'll never please a guy.'

And there was this one. Surprisingly this one reappeared in my mind only recently. If I looked through my high school photos, I could probably find these girls' names. Quite frankly, they don't deserve recognition. I have no idea what was in the container they had, the very one they tried to pass off as mine.

I will call the first girl Tracy and the second one Morgana, as in the evil sorceress from Arthurian literature. While this girl was a witch, giving her the title of a sorceress would be insulting to the real Morgana.

Tracy appeared in 1989 and we connected quickly. She was nice, caring and listened to me. I thought I had finally found a friend and, I enjoyed going to school for the first time in my life. It lasted only one term.

Morgana showed up. To say she stole Tracy from me is

most likely a lie, but it felt that way. I wrote a note to Tracy in the hopes she would read it alone. They were inseparable and I didn't want Morgana to know. (*How naïve I was.*) I basically told Tracy, 'What did I do wrong? I thought we were friends.' Not in those words, but something along those lines.

They never approached me during school. I was waiting for mum to pick me up after school, in a shady area on the other side of the road from the school gates. I saw the two of them exiting the gates carrying a cooking tin with a towel over it. They had to cross the zebra crossing to get to me, sniggering and snickering as they walked. They approached, indicating the tin belonged to me. Something about its contents can only cause monobrows. I did have what looked like a monobrow at that time. They placed it at my feet. As much as I tried to ignore them, turning to look down the street or up it, they would move to meet my gaze. All I wanted was for mum to come to the rescue; drive up to provide me escape. Naturally, she only arrived after they started walking away. The tin stayed on the side of the road.

I was very sporty at school and tried to join as many teams as I could. Sport is supposed to bring people together in peace and harmony. How can a team of players be nasty? We were doing softball tryouts for the teachers to pick the right players to create a team. Several of the girls trying out were telling me how hopeless I was, not being good enough to make the cut. I tried ignoring them, but they made sure I heard them, facing me and speaking aloud — obviously not loud enough for the teacher to tell them to stop. If she heard and ignored it, she was a bad teacher.

When it was my turn to 'batter up', I grabbed the bat, placed my feet firmly near the base, raised the whacking device over my shoulder and faced the pitcher. In an instance, I plastered every one of their faces on that ball. I guess creating an imaginary friend helped with the ability to do this effectively. As it sailed towards me, all my rage, all my anger, moved my arms forward with such speed that the bat hit the ball hard. That white little leather clad sphere soared. I swear I saw the afterburner fire exhaust. The 'bat quake' rippled up my arms, sending a quivering sensation throughout my body. It became my technique to always hit a home run. I made the cut. Don't think they were happy.

The last memory I have of this school was when I won the Courtesy Award, albeit my tuckshop payback was anything but courteous. When I went to accept the award at the office, the principal — the same one who didn't care if I failed subjects other than religion — told me, 'I don't think I should give this to you, considering what I have heard.'

'What was that?' I asked.

She rattled off some lecture about what I supposedly did, but I knew she was incorrect. I told her as much. She never apologised for making the error and seemed to give me the award reluctantly. The next day at assembly she used the construction site as an analogy for someone's reputation. 'A person's reputation is like a construction site, easy to tear down, difficult to rebuild.' (*This can equally be applied to faith, trust, love — all the above*). Not sure if any of the bullies understood her message. They still hounded me. But boy, did I feel embarrassed. I knew she was referring to the rumours ruining my reputation.

When I finally left that school and moved to a state school, I found I couldn't quite figure out where to go. I had three separate groups to consider joining for lunch. One group, I quickly disliked. They didn't make me feel right. They were nice but their attitude felt more rebellious in nature, like they loved breaking the rules. At least, that was the impression I got.

The second group sat under a covered awning near the Year Twelve rec room. They were okay. But they often talked about parties they had over the weekend, parties I was never invited to. It seemed they didn't want to include me in anything. And thinking further, I don't think they engaged in conversation with me unless I initiated it.

One day they decided to play football. It was supposed to be 'touch'. This is what they told me. I believed them, didn't I? When the ball was passed to me, I got tackled. I heard laughter. I wasn't embarrassed or ashamed, mostly shocked. The guy on top of me (*I think he was the first male to have bodily contact with me*), helped me up, asked if I was okay and apologised. Perhaps he was trying to tell me something, like maybe he was interested in me. He never said anything. But actions can speak louder than words. I obviously didn't get the translation. It could have been rough play. Boys will be boys, right? My arm hurt due to breaking the fall, but it wasn't broken. It hurt enough to stop me playing though.

The last group was a trio of girls. I didn't have much to do with two of them and vice versa, but Angel (*fake name, but she was an angel*) and I got on like a house on fire. They were in one of my science classes. I kept my distance from them at first because they looked like the type of girls who would make the other school's bullies look like lollipops. The term 'bitch' passed my mind many times. Knowing how I hated that term, why did I use it? Simple. I had no other word to use other than bully, yet that word seemed too weak.

One day, when walking to class, one of them dropped a book. I picked it up and called out to them. 'Excuse me, I think you dropped this.' And in that one instance, we were able to talk to each other as friends. There was no bullying, no intention of bullying, no harassment and no fear of it ever happening. And the ironic thing is, they too thought I was a bitch, which is why they kept their distance from me.

Angel and I would tease each other with nicknames — she was SA, as in Smart Arse. Mine was MnM, as in Major Migraine. One day, walking between classes, I complained I was getting a migraine and she commented, 'You are a Major Migraine.' I looked at her and said, 'Smart Arse.' Every time we met, she greeted me as 'M'n'M' and I said, 'Ess Ay.'

Angel was the only reason I survived the last year of school. She made it tolerable. Unfortunately, after school, we drifted apart. I often wonder what happened to her. I think she ended up in Brisbane.

But to say the bullying stopped is not correct. At the end of the day on the very first day of school, I was walking to the bus stop. I had to go through an undercover area, a small room — think it contained lockers — and there were these younger boys playing with a tennis ball. They lost control of it as I passed. I didn't deliberately stop it — I would have, considering I am very courteous — but it hit my foot regardless. One of them yelled out, 'Did I give you permission to stop my ball you bitch?' I just kept walking.

Another incident happened around mid-year. I was walking to class and a guy said something nasty to me. Made me feel threatened. And I had the courage — a result of Angel's friendship — to tell him off. He said, 'I know [name omitted]. I know you work for him. I'm going to get you fired for that.'

Whether he did know the owner of where I worked is anyone's guess. But as I was bullied in there too, I didn't quite mind getting fired. I replied with a smile, 'Be my guest.' It didn't have the effect he was seeking and I continued to my class.

There probably were a myriad other bullying incidents, but these are foremost in my mind. I didn't have a good time at school. Most people I met over the years loved going to school. I hated it, and I don't use that word lightly. One year it was extreme, to the point I made the decision to never have children. I couldn't fathom the idea of bringing a child into such a cruel and uncaring world.

Bullying belittles a person. It strips them bare of all human essentials, like the will to live. I read many stories of bullied kids who have taken their lives. It is a crime. Bullies need to be made accountable for their actions. Furthermore, parents of bullies need to be made accountable for their children's behaviour. Something needs to be done. For me, it is a little too late, which you will discover in due course.

But you can see a troubled mind, constantly bombarded with insecurities, insults, lack of appreciation and respect, can be damaged enough to allow figments of imagination to appear like real people. I only wished Angel came into my life from the very beginning. School life wouldn't have been so daunting and I would have kept the dream of having children of my own. Plus, I wouldn't have suffered an obsession due to an overactive imagination.

CHAPTER 3

Destroying a dream

Getting over that celebrity artist was one of the hardest things I have had to do. First loves are. It's worse when they don't even know you exist. And I did it alone. There was no one to help me with this. I didn't want anyone to know, keeping it to myself. I felt ashamed and didn't wish to share that emotion for fear someone would use it against me in another bullying fiasco. Bullying creates paranoia. Everything entering your life has this doubt lingering over it, as if advertising, 'will be used against you'. I got myself into this mess and it was up to me to get myself out of it.

My obsession followed me after graduation in 1992. It was constant. It was tormenting. It was torture. There was a guy in the world my heart was set on and I couldn't even meet him or let him know. I would come across as nutty as a fruit cake. It wasn't him. But it felt real despite only being a fantasy with his face on it. It was why I had to get rid of him from my mind. The idea reeked of insanity.

They came to Townsville once, performing in a nightclub. Was it an under-18s concert? Maybe, but it wouldn't have mattered. It was still a nightclub. My mother flatly refused to let me go. Naturally, I was angry and upset. I cried. My favourite band and I couldn't go see them. I felt my world being destroyed. (*Kids can be melodramatic.*)

Would meeting them have helped me? Doubt it. While no real person can stand up to a person's fantasies because figments of imagination are perfect, they have no flaws, I would have come across as a fan — an underaged and obsessed fan. There would have been no way he would have accepted me and being rejected wouldn't have helped my mental health.

In the end, my fantasy screwed me harder than bullying ever did. Yes, I screwed up. No, I didn't realise I was doing this. I was young and stupid. Does it make me sick today? No. It was a part of the growing up I needed to become the woman I am today. We learn by our mistakes. And this one had a harsh lesson: never fall in love with your own imagination. Or better yet, don't make imaginary friends.

I don't blame the artist. How could I? It wasn't his fault my troubled mind latched onto him. But releasing him from my mind took a lot of effort. And again, I can thank him for this. He got married. I was able to use that to my advantage, as painful as it was at the time.

I kept telling my mind, *he is no longer available*, and *you're old enough to know better* and *grow up for heaven's sake*. To say it worked quickly is a blatant lie.

It all started in 1989. By 1992 I was drowning within the obsession, it affected my life. I couldn't sleep, I couldn't eat properly, I couldn't focus, all I could think about was him. And I hated myself because I didn't have the guts to seek him out. And all the while I was hiding it from the world — another mistake. Had I reached out, the pain wouldn't have lasted as long.

Did I cry when he married? Probably. But I used it as a springboard to begin detoxing him from my system. I deliberately stopped myself seeking information about him. I tried finding hobbies or other things to do to take my mind off him.

The obsession made me insult myself. I became my own bully, saying things like *you're so stupid, he would never consider you* and *you're worthless* and *get over yourself already*. Despite insulting myself, I tried hard to move forward with my life. In between the meditations to remove the figment of my imagination, I tried the dating scene, which I discuss in detail in the next chapter. But as for the artist, I was methodically removing every fibre of his existence from my life as best as I could. Piece by piece I removed his essence from my troubled mind.

I thought I was winning the battle when little snippets of him entered my life. To avoid any possible identification, I won't say what these were but there was enough to undo my efforts. When I found these little treasures of information, I would revert to seeing him before me, not all the way to the beginning, but it did set me back somewhat. It was a constant battle. Fighting the injuries caused by the bullies was easier. Why? Because it was love.

I was fighting love, not insults. And to be honest, it wasn't love for him. It was lust. Lust is far more powerful than love. It drives you to do stupid things — like conjure up hallucinations and stick real faces on them. True, the apparition was there long before he entered my life but creating the beast in the first place was stupid.

Eventually, around 1996, I finally found peace. I wasted seven years of my life on an obsession, on someone who doesn't know I exist. And the final four years were excruciating. I felt I was suffocating. But in the end, I won. At least I thought I did. Do you ever get those moments when you think back to your past and wonder, 'Hmm, what ever happened to them?' Silly me did this. But in my defence, it wasn't entirely my fault. I had a dream about him. The only thing from this dream which stuck was his face. I didn't wake up feeling loved or having been loved proving intimacy was not involved. It was as if he came calling to say, 'Hey, long time no see.'

And stupid me makes the silly mistake of looking him up on the internet. 'What's wrong with that?', you might ask. It came with an image. He's still devastatingly handsome.

It brought all the emotions, all the feelings, all the stupidity back to my mind. For context, at the time I didn't have anyone in my life to love other than my mother and a dog. No friends, no relationships, nothing. There was a part of me that desired it but, thanks to my experiences, I feared seeking it. That doesn't mean I can't feel those feelings. And seeing him again, brought them all to the surface.

Do I regret it? No. I might be a little ashamed, but it was what I did and now I must deal with it. Besides, while I appreciate him, I am not fantasising about him anymore. I don't call one-off dreams fantasies. I was asleep. I don't have control of my subconscious when I am unconscious. They are simply memories resurfacing for some reason. Decoding them is the challenge. The only thing I can do today is deal with the shame of my youthful stupidity.

I'm sure he won't appreciate what I have done here, nor would I expect him to. I hope I don't meet him because I'm sure he'll see the shame in my eyes. And to be honest, I don't know if I could face him. Would he insult me? I think I'd be devastated. Would he understand? I don't know. I fear finding out. And I don't do well with confrontation. It paralyses me.

I was at the bank after the second Covid outbreak in 2021 when we were all required to wear masks. There was a guy in front of me with two young children, a guy sitting on a couch, and there was this arsehole at the back without a mask. The couch guy and maskless guy were in a conversation.

'You must be one of them dickheads who disobeys the rules,' couch guy said. 'You need to wear your mask.'

'I don't have to wear a mask, jackass.' Maskless man smirked.

The father turned around and shouted, 'We're all wearing masks, mate, and you need to wear yours. You ain't gonna spread this to us. Do as you're told.'

The maskless guy swore at him, forcing the father to approach him threateningly, stating that his language was not tolerated as he had two young kids with him, and they didn't need to hear it. His voice was high, stern and ferocious.

And there I was, standing in line while all this exploded around me, with my mind shouting, 'Get the hell out of here.' I probably would have if I could have felt my legs. I was frozen. I broke out in a sweat and found difficulty breathing — not because of the mask, because confrontation affects me that way. There is the fight or flight instinct in all of us. Mine is the 'duck and hide', and I couldn't even do that. My legs failed to respond to all commands.

Confrontation and I don't get along. This is the result of all those years being bullied and unable to defend myself adequately, injustices suffered through work and other forms of torment life threw at me. It manifests into a paralysing fear. If the artist did meet with me to antagonise me, I wouldn't be able to flee, even if I wanted to.

Why would he antagonise me? My paranoia is dictating this. Can you blame me? Everyone I met has dug a blade in my back in one way or another. Meeting anyone has a lingering doubt clouding it. The artist could be a jerk for all I know, or he could be the sweetest angel to ever grace the Earth. I will never know. How could I approach a guy who doesn't know me and say, 'Hey, I used to fantasise about you.' I can see him bolting away like the Road Runner, or perhaps call the police and slap a restraining order against me.

Despite this fear hounding my thoughts, I would like to give that artist a big hug (*if appropriate*) and thank him:

> You don't know me. And I'm sorry I latched onto you in my youth. I tried hard to mask your identity here, in respect of your privacy. I hope no one figures you out because it might cause you grief. Not my intention. You helped me in ways no one ever could, even if it was only my own imagination working against me.
>
> It may have only been a dream, but it felt real. And to my troubled mind, it was real. Enough to keep me away from suicide at least.
>
> Celebrities don't realise how deeply they can affect people. It is amazing how they can help people without even knowing. Thank you for that, at least.
>
> The flip side to it all is, people don't understand that celebrities want to be treated like everyone else. And my stupid youth denied this for you. For this, I apologise. I wish you the very best.

CHAPTER 4

A journey through the land of perplexing men

'You had me thinking it was like a fleet.' Who said this? Oh right, Richard (Tom Selleck) from *Friends*. When undertaking this journey, I believed I only dated enough guys to count them all on one hand. I discovered there were those who slipped the memory bank and resurfaced as I tried hard to remember details. There were eight in total. Not sure this would be classified as a fleet, maybe it would if they were ships. But as they weren't all kisses and sex, we can dismiss a few as simple encounters. And even if I could name them all, only a few names come to mind. But I'm using fake names, does it really matter?

If you're thinking this sex story is going to be juicy, you can forget it. (*I have a few details, but girth isn't included.*) It is daunting enough to be talking about this stuff — to add deeper and more compounding detail would simply be too embarrassing (*puns intended*).

To them, this will be quick and painful. To me, I'll be glad to get it over and done with. But it is my story. And I know not all men are uncaring idiots, but these are the encounters I experienced. Plus, I promised you a sex tape of sorts.

My first kiss

I knew this guy because my parents were friends with his. In all the years we met I never thought we would be dating. Then 1994 springs to mind, but don't quote me on it. Despite this book being a memoir, most of these memories are blended. I cannot discuss how our relationship started but I know we dated.

His name was Pluto (*the Roman myth, not the Disney dog. Not sure he'll appreciate that name, but like I said in the prologue, these names are not designed to give meaning to who they are; it is to identify them within the story.*) He was kind and thoughtful. In the beginning. Not sure if he got bored with me or I simply didn't 'do it' for him, but he didn't fight for me when I said my final goodbye. He simply said, 'Okay.'

What killed it for me was something he did that was thoughtless, full of selfishness and damn near made me so angry I wanted to tear his skin off and hit him with it. Not the exact thought you should have about someone you are supposed to love.

He was my first kiss. The first time my lips touched another set of lips. The first time my tongue explored a foreign mouth. It was all consenting. It wasn't planned, it came out of nowhere. It was at the house where he rented. He had two rooms: a bedroom and a computer room. I never saw his bedroom. This event happened in the other room. And that kiss was warm, nice and ... I wish it never happened. The result. My God, the result.

A week after the intimate encounter, I started feeling a little under the weather. A cloggy nose, a cloggy head, sore throat and difficulty breathing because I had to breathe through my mouth, which resulted in dry cracking lips. When I called him, he said, 'Boy, you don't sound good.' (*Thanks for stating the obvious.*)

'I'm not.' I responded with a nasal drawl. (*Like, duh!*) 'When we kissed, did you have a cold?'

'Yep.' He sounded proud, like he had conquered me through inflicting me with a disease. Like it was the best thing he could ever do. Like he didn't care.

How do you like that? My first kissing encounter and the scoundrel couldn't consider my health. 'Sorry sweety, I'm not feeling well. Let's do this another time.' How difficult is it to say this?

Perhaps I am overthinking it. I don't mind sharing, but germs are one thing that should remain yours. Don't share them around. Not everyone enjoys being sick.

He didn't consider the health aspects of the whole shebang.

He wanted the kiss; it was more important to him than anything. To me, this was a lack of respect. A lack of courtesy. A lack of love. And it proved men only wanted one thing.

One day, he told me, 'Your mother is negative.'

What does that say about me? If he couldn't respect my mother, it translates to disrespecting me. Why? Because she gave birth to me, I love my mother and feel insulted when others bad mouth her. It was like he attempted to hurt me by going through her. What did he really think of me if he thought I came from negativity?

In the end, I couldn't respect him. He deliberately made me sick and he had no nice words about my mother. In the end I became unhappy and knew it wasn't going to work out. I had to dump him. And I think he was happy to see me go. Think it only lasted a couple of months. But I did get something out of the relationship. He introduced me to both *Blackadder* and *Red Dwarf*. I love these shows.

In the end, my prelude to a sexual encounter gave me a disease. Yes, I know there are risks, but it shouldn't happen right out of the gate. What would the next guy do? Was this to be the foundation of attitude from all men? Were they all scumbags? It certainly marred my entry into the world of romantic interactions.

My first time

For the record, Janus was an interesting man. To avoid exposing the real him, I can't say much, but he did have a life of adventure. He was older than me by at least ten years. And I know he had a business venture that went bust — or was it an investment? And he once said he was involved in a project he wasn't allowed to talk about because he signed a non-disclosure statement. Not sure why he said this, probably hoping I'd sleep with him for information. But for the most part, he was a gentleman. For the most part.

The year 1995 springs to mind. Mind you, all these memories are mixed, as if my mind placed them in a blender and instructed me to guess. He worked in retail, at a store I visited often. To avoid identification, I won't name which one but I was interested in their products. I wasn't rude, neither was he. We would greet each other with a courteous and friendly 'hello'.

Eventually he gathered the courage to ask me out. I always said he was the first man to ask me out, the first one who was interested, because I pursued the others. But to say I slept with him straight away would be untrue.

Janus had a lot of words in him but they felt more rehearsed than from the heart. At least it sounded that way. He told me once, 'A psychic told me I'd meet someone in Townsville. I guess she was right.' Was this supposed to be a pick-up line or a compliment? I didn't take it as either.

And as for the sex? Well, I think we were dating for about

four months before the event came around like a slow-motion plane crash. It was at his place. I was spending the night. It was my intention to lose my virginity. I wanted it. I needed it. My body demanded the experience. I felt I deserved it after years of neglect. However, my heart and mind should have chosen someone else.

It was a weekend in 1996, but don't ask me the date. Can anyone really recall the exact date they lost their virginity? Given my experience, I wish I could forget the entire fiasco. It wasn't a quick, wham bam thank you ma'am event. He did take his time. He ensured I was comfortable. He did foreplay, if one could call it that — he could have been a lot better at it. Before too long, he was in me. There was no clock to count the seconds or minutes — if we even got that far. When he was done, he rolled over, gave me his back, and went to sleep.

And there I was. Lying in his bed. Naked. Staring into the darkness trying to see the ceiling patterns. And my mind was screaming, 'Hey! Where are the fireworks?'

My first kiss gave me a disease and my first time made me feel empty. There wasn't even a desire to want more or seek it. I felt flat. I think if I still possessed an imaginary friend, it would have deflated him too. But hell, I think the fantasy would have at least made the sex more interesting. Come on, leave me my delusions.

I will share this though, even if it embarrasses me. I experienced my first sixty-nine position. I didn't think it was anything special, hence why he could have been better. But the next day I could barely speak. Wasn't sure that's usual by doing that kind of thing. I did it one more time years later with someone else and never got a sore throat. But when I confronted him on it, he advised, 'I don't wash it because I hate the way the soap makes my skin feel.' Or some similar rubbish. Here was more proof some men don't care about women's health when it comes to sex. It needs to be clean if it's going inside a woman's body. Dirt inside the vagina equates to bacteria and disease. No wonder women are suffering with cervical cancer.

Yet I didn't let this bad sex ruin the relationship. I stayed with him. I think we 'played' a few more times, I never counted how many. He probably had a tally. I wanted to pursue a long-term relationship. It was the norm, wasn't it? Everyone was doing it. Some naïve part of me thought his performance might get better. Ha! What a joke. But it all came crashing down on one fateful Friday.

My sister held a party at her place. He was supposed to pick me up at 5:30 pm. My parents left at around 5 pm. They offered to take me, but I told them, 'Janus said he'd pick me up. I'll wait for him.'

And boy did I wait; 5:45 pm came and went, testing my patience like it was poking it with a stick. Six o'clock passed like a slow-moving freight train. The stick turned into an electrified cattle prod as the quarter hour approached. And my patience zapped away by 6:20 pm before he rocked up behaving like nothing was amiss. And in all this time spent waiting not one single phone call to let me know he was running late. His reason for the delay?

'Had a sale I couldn't get out of.'

Not even for a minute to give me a call and let me know he'd be late?

He could have done it, pretending to call a supplier or something. The client didn't need to know he was showing respect to his girlfriend. Had he done this, I would have told him to meet me at the party and got my parents to take me. But no. He wanted to make me wait. I lost all respect for him because it felt as if he had none for me.

Am I wrong to think this way? Do you like waiting for lovers? A little courtesy goes a long way and this guy fell flat on his delivery. Perhaps I should have seen it coming. After all, he did make me wait for fireworks in bed. I never got them.

It spoiled everything for me. A long-term relationship with this guy was never going to happen. How many times would he leave me waiting without a phone call? And if you think I am being stupid, wait until you hear about his new car purchase (*later*).

I couldn't stand his lack of courtesy, his lack of respect. What does it matter if he fucked me (*sorry for the language*)? Did that mean he could stop respecting me? How would our lives be with me constantly waiting for him? I couldn't fathom that future. It's bad enough waiting in line at the bank. I saw no alternative but to dump him. Told him, it wasn't working out. (*Oh, the irony. Wait for this one.*)

Part of me wanted to get him to work on the problem, but here comes that brilliant piece of paranoia inflicted in me from all those years of bullying. Paranoia dictated that leopards don't change their spots and tigers don't change their stripes. It was all my mind needed to say, 'Sorry, goodbye'.

What it exposed was another interesting little behaviour he possessed. In our six months of dating, he would call about once or twice a week. No harm in that really, but when we broke up it was nearly every day. At least it felt like it. Every call, he would say the same old boring line, like it was a biblical mantra, as if he was indoctrinating the words into me and hoping they would grab, take hold of my brain, shake it, and change my mind.

'I love you. We're going to get married. We'll live in this big house. We'll have all these kids.'

He must have thought it was romantic. But how he spoke it, with a drawl and hardly any emotion attached to the words, my mind interpreted it like this: 'You are mine. I will chain you. I'll give you a lot of work to keep you busy. You won't have any freedom.'

His words were hollow. They sounded false and rehearsed. And despite him repeating them over and over and his big claim of love, when he finally left Townsville for another city in 1997, he called to say this: 'Got a job down south, I'll be leaving tomorrow.'

But that was all. A phone call, nothing more. No visit, no coming over to give a proper goodbye. If he truly loved me, wouldn't he have at least done that? Isn't that courtesy in action or am I being unreasonable? Does it matter? He left and I thought I was finally rid of him — until he called three months later. Thankfully my answering machine took the call. I didn't want to speak with him.

And, after three months' silence with no communication whatsoever, this is all he had to say: 'Hey, it's me. I just saw a show. Watch the *Vicar of Dibley* because I think it's funny. Bye.'

Consequently, I never watched the show. I'm sure it was funny. Hilarious even. But he marred any enjoyment I would ever get from it because I would be thinking of him when it came on. Not exactly what I wanted to do.

Later that same year, he called again. I answered it because I thought it might be a job prospect. How disappointed I was to hear his voice. I hardly said a word. He was all talk. And he made it sound like nothing had happened between us whatsoever. The conversation bored me out of my mind. I had to excuse myself, faking a bladder emergency and hung up. I never heard from Janus again, not until after meeting someone new and I was chatting online.

It was 1999 when he wanted to get back in touch. I was in desperate need of a friend, but I had this strange feeling — The Force in action perhaps — he was after more than I could provide. And I told him.

'I could always have another friend in my life, Janus, but that's all I can offer you. I cannot give you what you seek.'

CHAPTER 4   *A journey through the land of perplexing men*

It might have been cold-hearted to blurt something like that out, but I had to be honest. I don't like being misled, why would I do it to someone else?

However, I made the mistake of joining him to my chat with the person I was involved with at the time. And he was 'if you hurt her, I will find you,' type aggression. I had to boot him out. I think he was trying to show his chivalrous side; it came across as a stark-raving jealous rage.

Many years later, long after that other person and I parted ways, he connected with me again. This time, he was living somewhere else. I thought long and hard about when this happened. I was living at my parents' place and I drove from there to the restaurant and back again. But there was a time I lived alone in another suburb before relocating back to my parents' house. My gut tells me this occurred before my 'living alone' years but after the breakup with that other person. That leaves late 2001 to 2003, but I cannot pinpoint which year exactly. (*Sorry.*)

This day, he had bought a new vehicle in Brisbane. He flew there to collect it and drove back. We arranged to have lunch on his way through Townsville. I was to meet him at a restaurant at 12:30 pm. Knowing what he did to me in the past, I half expected him to be late and took a book with me. It didn't matter if he was late or not, I planned to make an afternoon for myself.

I was sitting there, with the book on the table. I ordered a beverage (*mint coffee, beautiful*) and waited. Twelve-thirty was only five minutes away. I always arrive early, no matter where I am going. When 12:45 pm passed without Janus in sight I started reading my book. (*Don't ask which one, I have no idea. I should, considering it would have been more interesting than waiting for him.*) When I saw 1:00 pm arrive on the clock, I ordered lunch and ate alone. I was out of there by 2 pm. He never showed. I had a basic mobile with no internet connection, and he had my number. He never phoned. (*Big surprise.*)

I got home, accessed my computer and there, like a little tiny bit of cheese tormenting a mouse, sitting in my email's inbox, was a message from him.

'Not gonna make it. Sorry. — Sent from my smartphone.'

Okay. He sent me an email — from his phone. He had my number. What was wrong with calling me? If he had to touch his phone to send an email, it would have been simpler to dial a number. Did he want to inflict the same pain on me as he did all those years ago? It didn't work. I learnt my lesson last time. And what's worse is that he didn't think he did anything wrong. Acted as if nothing happened. Guess my paranoia was correct when it told me leopards don't change their spots.

He moved to Townsville about a year later because he, 'wanted to be with me', despite me telling him from the start of our reignited friendship, 'I cannot give you what you seek.' And considering he stood me up — without a courtesy call — why would I bother with him?

I only met him twice while he stayed here. I had my own life and agenda to focus on. Most of it was spent in self-inflicted solitary confinement simply because I didn't want anyone in my life. I was satisfied with my solitude.

One day I sent him an email. No reply. A month later, I followed it up. No reply. Tried a third time. Nothing. As he was being childish, I gave up and continued with my life. About two years later, when I had a Facebook account, he befriends me, sending me an email. I replied, asking where he has been as I had been trying to get in touch. His response: 'I moved to New South Wales because I couldn't wait for you anymore.'

Was it my fault he kept ignoring my honesty that I couldn't give him what he sought? I knew it was what he wanted — The Force served me well. I was happy to have him as a friend, but I knew him too well. It was why I was trying to be honest. After his treatment, I didn't want romance or a relationship.

He obviously forgot the words I told him, or he simply ignored them; his selfish pride dictating to him he could change my mind. And I called him on it.

'I told you I couldn't give you want you wanted. I told you all I wanted was a friend. Is it my fault you didn't understand?'

There was no more communication. It proved men who sleep with women simply cannot be friends with them. Yet my sister hangs out with her boyfriend's ex-wife and ex-girlfriend. How the hell do they do it?

Yet this did not end the Janus interaction. During one of my paranoia-twisted, loneliness-induced depression bouts — probably three years after he finally stopped communicating, I placed a statement on my Facebook's wall. It read as follows:

'If I told you I was going to die tomorrow, what would you do?'

Deep stuff. Meaningful stuff. Dangerous stuff, especially when three out of the four replies I received thought I was crying out for help and contemplating suicide again. It was a test. I wanted to see how many of the fifty friends in my Facebook account practiced what they believed, what with all the uplifting and friendship message notes they circulated. I wanted to see if they were real friends and humanitarians.

Why do this? Well, when you send a person-to-person email/message via Facebook to a friend, you expect a reply. Of all the email messages I sent to people, I never received anything. Where is the connectivity? I tested them by uploading to my wall for all to see. And out of fifty, only four responded to my test. Yes, Janus was one of them. His response was, 'I'd start talking to you again.'

What the hell? He couldn't be bothered talking to me when I was alive and suddenly he wants to speak when I only have twenty-four hours left to live. Why would I waste my last breath on someone who simply didn't communicate with me when I was living? To me, it was an empty response.

Considering only four out of fifty responded to such a deep and dangerous sentence, I lost all faith and trust in Facebook. I killed the account. It was a sort of abuse — silence might be golden, but when you expect a reply or response, silence is as good as a dagger in the back. I have never invested in social media again. What's the point? Especially if there is no connection.

As for Janus, he was my first. I lost my virginity to someone who, thinking back, did not deserve to have it. And I hope virgins reading this will learn from my lesson. Don't be hasty to give it away. You need the right person. They need to know what you need and understand that a virgin's first encounter must be as magical as possible (*if they exist*). Mine? Was as flat as a pancake, and that's insulting to the dessert. Pancakes are sweeter. Maybe it was like a flat tyre.

The ones that didn't make the cut

I dated five other guys — if you could call them dates — one before Pluto and four after Janus. The years, months, days are all over the place, making putting this in chronological order difficult, but I'll give it a shot.

The one before Pluto was a school friend. He was the first guy I dated. I wrote a note to him in class explaining how I felt about him. I had no idea how to approach someone and express face to face how I felt (*a sorry trait that would follow me like a plague*). Can you blame me? All my face-to-face interactions were with bullies. Would he point his finger and laugh? Would he incite others to make fun of me? It was all too much to consider and, to be honest, I didn't even know how he felt about me. Furthermore, I didn't think it would work.

Surprisingly, he took the note and accepted me. We went on a few dates, movies mainly. Not sure if I kissed him but I did go to the prom with him.

Loki (*probably not a name I should apply to him*) showed me how to get money back from public phone booths via a signal sent by keying in numbers in a specific order, hanging up, dialling his number, having the conversation, hanging up and the money returned — or did he have another code to enter? At first, I thought it was a magic trick, you know sleight of hand, but it turned out to be real. That scared me because it was a crime. I couldn't deal with the thought of breaking the law. It would have been a shadow choking my thoughts, my feelings, my every move. I even felt the glare of police on me, and they weren't even around. It affected my feelings for him and our relationship fell apart.

The first of the four after Janus I will name as Tatius. He was a university friend. A few memories exist of him, but not many. I felt good around him and with him, feeling safe and accepted. He fainted in our hallway once. Dad had to carry him to the lounge. He was on antidepressants and thought he could stop them cold turkey. He found out the hard way this was not the case. We had to call his parents to come and get him.

He introduced me to a cartoon called *Daria*. I see a lot of her in me, except my voice is more like a cross between Jane and Brittany. I still watch this show today.

He didn't want me to cut my hair, even to trim it to help it grow. Or perhaps I misunderstood him? No, I didn't, because I thought that was a little weird and possessive. Seriously, how dare someone tell you that you cannot have a haircut. I understand movie stars are often restricted with this, at least I was told as much when going for a costume fitting after winning an audition. The girl said, 'Oh, you cut your hair. You're not actually meant to do that without getting permission first.' I believe that was why I didn't get the part. They were expecting long hair. Strange though as the agent I signed up with never mentioned I would need permission.

No memory comes forward about kissing Tatius. We laid together on my bed once. I think our intimacy was simply closeness and touch. But this is all I can remember.

About number two after Janus, I won't say much of what he does, because honestly, he doesn't deserve the recognition, but I'm sure he isn't the only guy who does this. This encounter was brief, it can't be classified as a proper date.

It was probably a month after I dumped Janus. I believe they were friends because he mentioned Janus — wait for it. We went to a restaurant, we had a meal, he wanted to know if I had seen Townsville at night at the top of Castle Hill — a tourist lookout; someone told me it's the plug for a large extinct volcano (*at least we hope it's extinct*). As I had never had the opportunity, he offered to take me up there. Not trusting him fully, I said, 'I'll follow you.'

Yes, I drove myself to this 'date'. He didn't pick me up, although he probably would have wanted to. Thank God, I didn't let him.

At the top of the hill, magical as it looked, he went in for a kiss. Not a peck, not on the cheek, a full-on passionate kiss smack bang on the lips. He didn't even ask, simply moved in. I baulked and backed away.

'What are you doing?' I asked, shock filling my tone like a flood.

'Did Janus hurt you that much, did he?' he asked.

I think he was smiling, probably in anticipation he was going to win.

'I'm sorry, I'm not ready for that.'

True, I wasn't ready. I had recently come out of a relationship. And I don't give out on the first date anyway. Yet one more memory is going to make me regret these words.

As for this guy, he sulked. I couldn't believe it. He stopped talking, wouldn't make eye contact. When he left, I heard his car skidding out of the area, like a bat out of hell.

What the hell? Sure, there are women out there who might give out on the first night, but I'm not one of them. If he knew Janus, he would have known. I didn't kiss Janus right away either. And considering he knew Janus and contacted me very quickly after I dumped him, I can only assume Janus divulged private information to him and he wanted a piece of the cake. That doesn't bode well for the trust-building skills. I never saw or heard from him again.

I wish I could recall more memories about the next guy in this group. He was a nice guy, but his driving left much to be desired. Being in the car with him was like taking a bungie jump off a bridge with a shoddy rope. It was erratic and scared the hell out of me. I'm a cautious driver. He made Le Mans look docile. He took me up Mount Stuart, another lookout at the other end of town from Castle Hill. He had to fill up with gas because he forgot to do it earlier in the day.

In all the time I was with him, he never kissed me, never forced himself on me and never made a move. He was simply being out with me, enjoying the night and company. One night, I had such a nice time, I felt elevated. By the time he got me home and wished me goodnight, I French kissed him. This apparently took him by surprise, but he reciprocated. I know I went out with him a few times, but the relationship only lasted a few weeks.

What ended it though had nothing to do with him. He was a really nice guy, and I did like him. But I couldn't lead him on and waste his time. Since dumping Janus, I began a soul-searching crusade, seeking the answer as to why I couldn't find a guy who curled my toes or made my soul dance. Possibly I was aiming too high, but the guys I met didn't even raise a bubble to my feelings — although this guy almost made the mark because of how he treated me. To my surprise, I found the answer. And it came before I met this guy. While he wasn't my last, he certainly proved the answer was correct, because even though that kiss was nice, it didn't do anything for me.

Before I divulge the answer, let me tell you about the last guy belonging to this group. I know the encounter occurred before 2001. I'm thinking 1998 because in 1999 my situation changed. I met him through a work acquaintance.

A little background story — I worked at a bakery in one of the supermarkets. Part of the uniform included an apron. There was this colleague who had the nasty habit of teasing me by always pulling my apron strings open. I was constantly having to stop what I was doing to refasten them. To say it was annoying was a major understatement. The more I asked her to stop, the more she did it. School flashback. She wouldn't stop if I simply asked, forcing me to resort to my high school English skills and use a dash of reverse psychology on her.

One day, she did it again, looking back at me as she walked off with a smile. I approached her, doing it up again, and made sure my glare reached through her eyes and into her soul, not in a menacing kind of way, but more seductive. And I said, teasingly, 'Careful, you might turn me on.'

Unsurprisingly, she never undressed me again. But it didn't ruin our friendship. She invited me to a party one weekend. In those days, I had a bit of a social scene, if I could call it that, and at this party was this guy. A dead ringer for Billy Zane, the actor who was in the film *The Phantom*. The eyes, the smile, his behaviour. Crap! Maybe it was Billy (*Relax. It wasn't.*)

I was immediately attracted to him but tried hard to hide my feelings. Why? Because they were conflicted. I wanted something else, but he was pulling at my heartstrings, hard. I guess he was smitten from the word go. Either that or I was the next conquest on his list. I don't know, but his flirtations were relentless.

One part of me is saying this occurred at another party, a second encounter. But another part is slapping me in the face and telling me it happened on the first meeting. I always believed I never gave out anything leading to sex on a first encounter. But if this was the first night, it makes me a hypocrite. Never thought I would be one of those. This is the memory that makes me regret saying, 'I never give out on the first encounter'.

His flirting was unyielding. And I reciprocated because he was inciting passion within me. Why did I flirt back? My thoughts and emotions were clashing. The answer I found couldn't be the answer I needed, surely. Perhaps he was a last-ditch effort to prove the answer was either true or false. Heck, he even did a handstand, as if that was going to turn me on. I think I was turned on before he did that. Maybe he was indicating he was head over heels, or is that heels over head? It was in his case.

We ended up pashing in his bedroom. He tried desperately to find a condom. And we engaged in coitus. We were in there for some time. However, I am unable to provide you any more context or how it felt because another memory of him always takes precedence, as if telling me, 'Forget the sex, this is what he is.'

On another date, he asked if it was okay to check on a friend of his. I thought, 'Sure.' (*I want to go back in time and slap myself in the face.*) He wasn't going there to check up on a friend. He was going there to light a bong and do a marijuana deal. And here I was in the same room, with a lit bong, smoke filling my lungs and my head starting to spin. I didn't inhale from the bong. I didn't need to. The smoke did a number on my head by itself. And to make matters worse, he drove me home under the influence of drugs. During the drive, he was boasting about how much he made weekly on the deals. All I wanted was to get home and soak my head under a tap — or throw it down the toilet.

And as for the list of boyfriends, he was the last. Ended on a busted deal.

THE ONE I HAD ORDERS TO LET GO

This guy is the only one in the group who deserves a special mention. And I know people are going to go, 'Eww!' Why? He was a distant relative. (*Don't look at me like that please.*) I was in a real bad place, mentally and emotionally. It had been months since I had dumped Janus and was not long after the guy who couldn't accept no for an answer. It felt everything was against me and thus I fell into an abyss of depression. I'm surprised I even fell for this gentleman.

I will call him Evander. He deserves a reward for how he treated me. He was the living embodiment of a gentleman. He never forced himself on me — none of the guys I dated did, but the difference was, I wanted him to — not in a rape-me kind of way (*hell no!*), but in a sweep-me-off-my-feet kind of way. To take me unexpectedly. To surprise with love. It was something I expected Janus to do but never received it. And my body demanded it. I felt I deserved it; I was due for a reward, overdue even. But, as Evander was a gentleman, he never did. Maybe being related was holding him back? I don't know.

We began writing to each other. When I told him about Janus and the other guy, his support flowed like he had wrapped his arms around me. His words felt like he was holding me tight and reassuring me that everything was going to be all right. And with that, our letters became more and more intimate.

There was a passion in our words, but respect as well. Our love blossomed. When he came visiting (*will not divulge the year to avoid any identification of him — a few relatives have come visiting*), we were enraptured. There was an instant spark between us. I wanted to spoil him, to show him I loved and appreciated him.

And yes, we kissed. I kind of set the scene; he couldn't avoid it. I took him to a secluded area away from the city lights to see the Milky Way and stars in all their splendour. It was romantic, mesmerising, intense. He looked at me and smiled. The moment was passionate and it forced our lips together. Unfortunately, a car was being driven over a ridge in the distance, coming towards us, the headlights getting brighter. Evander got concerned — a response to the backpacker murders in Australia (1989 — 1993) — we left, and I took him to Castle Hill. I shouldn't have done this because of what the other guy did, but Evander made it magical.

His kiss still lingers in my mind. It was sensual. It was full of passion. I only wish we had more time. Mum found out and demanded I break up with him. There was no future in relatives getting together.

I was devastated. Had she not interfered, I believe I would have married him. If he wasn't related, mum would have allowed it. If anyone deserves happiness, it is him.

CHAPTER 5

The answer leads to ruin

I said, 'I couldn't lead the guy on'. After Janus, I undertook a deep investigation into my desires, my emotions, feelings, sensations, my likes and dislikes — what I needed in a partner and how to develop my search patterns to find a better loving half. I needed an answer to my problems and why I kept striking out with men. And to this day, it bugs me that despite finding it, I still slept with that drug dealer; like I had betrayed my real identity. It didn't come overnight. It was past my time with Evander when I found it. And it was blatantly obvious. Well, it was after I discovered it.

I found myself being attracted to women. It begged the question, *Why did I have sex with that drug dealer?*

The revelation I had lesbian tendencies shocked me at first but made a lot of sense. Women are sensual, sensitive, sexual. Men want sex *(although this excludes Evander. If he did want it, he never demanded it. Perhaps being related dictated his thoughts? But he kissed me, right?).* At least, this was my conclusion based on my experiences.

My lesbian encounters weren't many. There was the one I found through a newspaper personal advert; there was the soldier; there was another, whom I think was in the military; there was the teacher; there was Freya. Ah, dear, sweet Freya. She was very special. After her there was Larunda, Verdandi, and lastly, Maia. Remember, all fake names, in case you forgot.

Eight in total. A balance to the list of sexual encounters with men. But I only kissed and made love with one of the women — Freya. And she deserves a chapter all to herself. Larunda and Verdandi deserve separate chapters as well. Here I will discuss the others and how they affected, not only my life, but my opinions on the whole gay scene.

A lot of homosexuals might be wanting to rip my eyes out right about now, shouting, 'Being gay isn't a choice. We are born this way.' I've heard a few say this, not to my face mind you.

The way the world is going, it seems it is all screwed up. Everyone has their rights. Everyone demands them. Many homosexuals make excuses as to why they are what they are, not really knowing why they do what they do. I believe they are truly afraid of the truth, or fear they made a mistake. They don't need to fear anything but fear itself. When a gay person tells you, 'I was born this way' it is a lie. It sounds like they are blaming their parents when they say it. Their parents, after all, gave them life. No one is born any other way than as a blank slate. Let me explain:

A baby could be classified as non-binary because the baby's mind is blank. It has no conception of male, female or even non-binary. As the baby grows, it learns. The more it learns, the more it understands. Its personality, its likes and dislikes, form through parental guidance and upbringing, teachings at school and peer pressure from other kids who are simply trying to figure themselves out in the world. Their senses gather all the information, record their experiences and, like putty, mould them into the being they will become.

When puberty arrives, the hormones kick in hard. They are flooded with new emotions, feelings and desires. They learn about love and making love, passion and romance. They begin making decisions for themselves. Who they are attracted to, what turns them on, what turns them off etcetera etcetera. It is a conscious choice. Being gay is a choice. It is a life choice. I choose to be gay. I am not made gay; I am not born a lesbian. I choose to be one. I am in control of my destiny, no one else is, therefore it is my responsibility.

When someone tells you she or he is gay, that individual is telling you, 'It is my life, my choice, accept it.'

Why am I saying this? Because of my experiences. If I can choose to be gay, I can equally choose not to be. And I am not a lesbian anymore. At least, I don't think I am. I have not had a recent encounter with dreams or real people to decide otherwise.

I know life isn't as clear cut as I make it out to be, but my life is. I know there are people out there where the choice is forced on them, like an indoctrination-type influence. They still have the opportunity to discover this and make an informed decision as to whether they wish to continue or change. In the end, it is their choice.

These few encounters, lacking sex and kissing as they were, helped my decision in the end. Because a relationship is more than sex and kissing. It is a spiritual connection. It is an attraction beyond words. It is the ability to be close to someone and share life with them. I chose to be gay, I sought out lesbians and I had my encounters. I only wished they were different.

Newspapers sell emptiness

My first lesbian was found through a newspaper personal ad; hers, not mine. Not sure if they still exist, considering dating sites are available online these days.

It brings to mind a memory of personal ads, but unrelated to the meeting of this woman. One day, sitting in the lounge watching television, my brother-in-law (*well, ex-brother-in-law*) was perusing the newspaper and flipped to the personal advertisements. He was always such a tease when he was younger. He looked over to me, a sly smile on his lips, then back at the paper.

'Wait a minute,' he smirked. I could feel the joke brewing before he continued. 'I know that number.' He looked at me. 'It's yours.'

I glanced over at him, looked around for mum — she wasn't there — and leaned into him. 'Shush. Don't tell mum.' And this was my punchline to his joke. Of course, it wasn't my number, but I could tease him it was.

His eyes widened with shock. 'Seriously?' He couldn't believe it. I swear, I think he choked.

'Nah, gotcha.' I laughed. It took me a while to figure him out in the beginning, but once I found his joking manner, I kind of fed off it.

But this girl was no joke. She was about my age. And we arranged to go out. You would think I would remember my first ever lesbian date. But not one bit remains; I don't know where we went, I don't know what it was all about, whether we had lunch or dinner or walked around. As for her face . . . fitting, considering her name also escapes me. I sent a rose to her, a little gift of appreciation. And I know I must have had a good time and enjoyed her company because the following week, I called her to arrange another date. To say I was shocked by her response would be an elaborate fib. I was dumbfounded.

'Sorry, I've met someone else.'

Maybe I didn't spark the fire in her. How could I? I didn't know what the hell I was getting into, or what lesbians are expected to do on a first date. Do they meet, kiss, and enjoy the horizontal mambo straight away, or do they build up to it? I always thought it was the latter, perhaps I was wrong? Was I supposed to have sex with her in public? Or take her to a hotel? I have no idea.

I never saw her again. That's not to say I didn't hear from her. It was about two years later when she called out of the blue. Took me some time to sift through my memory to figure out who she was, but it was clear she wasn't calling for a date.

She told me that she had moved out of her 'overbearing' mother's house and found herself a nice place she was interested in obtaining. What she was after was the $10,000 deposit. I had to get her to repeat her request because I thought she was joking (*is there such a thing as candid telephone as opposed to camera?*) Did she really say that? Yep. I think my heart stopped, and not in a good way.

'How and why do you think I have that kind of cash?' I barked. 'And why the hell should I give it to you? I don't know who you are.'

Even if I did, I don't lend money to anyone. You never get it back.

She wasn't happy with my answer. Because we went on one date — if it could be called that — I had to fork over a fortune in cash? She wasn't an escort. We didn't have sex. Hell, I don't think we even kissed. And even if we did romp around, nowhere in her advert said I had to pay for anything.

Wasn't it a nice welcome into the world of lesbianism? Considering where the path led me, I should have cut and dashed right there, forgoing and forgetting my trek through the gay field of flowers. But a little voice in my head kept saying, 'Surely, they're not all like that.'

I wish I could put more context to the situation, but this is all I remember. It wasn't a good start. It made me feel perhaps I made a big mistake. But she was only one small fish in a large ocean of choices. I had to give my decision a chance to flourish. There were going to be mistakes along the path and I had to accept and deal with them as they arose.

East Timor protector

With this sweet beauty, her arrival in my life is vague. I know she came after the money-sucking leech. But there was another woman who I think was also in the military. Who came first? Not sure. But as I remember this sweet woman more clearly, I will deal with her first.

Names and faces are like dishes and spoons — they run away together. I think I was working at a bakery at the time because we arranged to meet late at night at her place after my shift ended, which was 10 pm.

One thing is clear, she was deployed to East Timor. It was around the time that Australia helped them from militia attacks. This gives me the year 1999. Don't think we communicated while she was there, but she told me before she left a package would be waiting for her to pick up. I simply offered my assistance.

Gasp! Shudder! I had no idea what the hell the package was, or what it contained. Could have been drugs for all I knew, even if it did come from one of those sport protein stores. I paid for it and picked it up. And I delivered it to her when she returned. Don't think she paid me back. I didn't care at the time. I still don't. It wasn't that much.

Why did I do it? Love makes you do stupid things. It blinds you to the rules. It blinds you to the risks. You simply want to please the person you're in love with, to show that person how much he or she means to you. It could have been sport protein, it could have been drugs. I'll never know.

These are the only memories I have of her. I can't even begin to think how it started or ended. Not sure if she was the woman whom I went to a gay bar with to enjoy a drink and dance, or if she was someone completely different. And that 'date' is the only memory I have of that person. It could have been a separate encounter; it might have been the East Timor protector. All I know is Ann Lee's *2 Times* was the song we danced to, and I purchased the single that week. I still have it.

Unknown brief encounter

This encounter was with a woman I barely remember. I think she had a crew cut, or short hair. She was a little muscular, which is why I think she too was in the military. Soldier comes to mind, but that might be the mixing of memories, blending all these women into one big cloggy bunch.

The only memory I have of her is being at her house and helping her bring the laundry in. Looking back at it, I think I came across as clingy. I think I was starting to get desperate and overdoing things or thinking too much about how I should be approaching women.

This encounter opened my eyes to my behaviour. This one wasn't good. I don't blame her for not wanting to be with me. I was clingy. I wanted to be around her, constantly. It was too much for her, obviously, because she didn't want anything more to do with me.

A person can be pushy to the extent that he or she pushes the object of his or her desire further from reach. People feel like they are being suffocated or trapped. People don't like that. I do feel a sense of remorse for my behaviour. If I had conducted myself better, who knows where it would have led.

And as I don't know her name — memories can be cruel — I cannot offer a sincere apology. If she is reading this and remembers me, I ask she forgives me. I hope she found the happiness she sought.

Teacher's unlikely pet

As for this one, what can I say? We met on several occasions. I even met her friends at her house for a dinner function. We played a mystery card game where I ended up being the killer. No one figured it out. It was fun and I wanted more. Sadly, no more would come.

Met her through a lesbian dating website. She didn't respond to my emails because her membership had expired. Thinking she might be the one, I gifted her a month's subscription.

She happened after my brief encounter, the one I pushed away with my clingy behaviour. I didn't want to come across as clingy with this woman. Perhaps I was playing it cool? Too cool for my own good, conceivably. I did enjoy her company. There is a memory of a pub meeting for lunch, which was fun.

She was a teacher but I'll reveal nothing more. Plenty of schools in Townsville, plenty of teachers too. There is a lot I remember about her but exposing it could well identify her and I am trying to avoid that. I can say she needed some stories for a project she was working on. I gave her some of mine. While she needed a lesbian theme, my stories may have been a little too pornographic for her liking. She didn't say anything. Not sure if she used any.

She provided me with some lesbian story books for my inspiration. It had been a long time since a teacher encouraged me to do something proactive. I think I may have read one or two short stories before I gave up because she lost interest in me. And I still have those books.

She may have been sincere when she accepted dating me or perhaps, she only went out with me to thank me for the subscription gift. I have no idea. It fizzled away to nothing. Not even sure if she still lives in town. I've never ventured back to her house to find out. I should go back one day, if only to return her books.

THE LAST LESBIAN

Maia was not the reason I stopped being a lesbian, but she did give weight to the decision. She was the very last woman I went out with. I cannot say we dated because, to me, it wasn't dating. It was enjoying the company of a friend.

She came into my life after Verdandi — more on her later. By the time I was done with Verdandi, I was in a state of mind where I believed I would never find true love and I would die alone. I had no interest in romance, sex, or any intimate connections. I had lost faith in the very concept of love and partnerships. All I needed was a friend.

The year was 2017. Like Verdandi and Larunda, I met Maia on a lesbian dating site. I was in the process of deleting my account. Having lost all faith in romance, I practically gave up searching. I was researching how to shut it down when a message popped up. Maia had contacted me. She was the first to issue a connection; all my other online contacts I had to instigate the first contact. Despite my mind settling in the 'I will be alone forever' ranch, chewing bits of straw, whittling on a piece of wood and feeling relatively comfortable, a part of me wanted to reach out to Maia to say, 'Thank you for noticing me.'

I'm not a rude person. When someone contacts me, I will respond. I answered her email but had to be honest. She had to understand my situation and what it meant for her.

'Listen,' I started, 'I'm at a time in my life I'm not interested in romantic or sexual encounters. My experiences have marred my emotions and I need to try to get them in order before I commit to anyone. I don't want to lead you on, and I don't want to waste your time. But if you can consider me a friend, I could use one right about now. If you don't reply, I will understand.'

Amazingly, she replied. Over the course of a few weeks, we bounced communication back and forth before arranging a meeting. We got along well, and I should congratulate her for her patience. We met a few times: lunches, coffees — would like to think I saw movies with her but I was turned off cinema due to the loud volumes. Last one I saw was with Verdandi. I spent a fair deal of time looking for a remote that didn't exist because the sound was piercing my ears. I ended up with a headache.

Maia wanted more than I could offer her. I often told her, 'If you find someone, I won't hold you back.' I think we saw each other for about four or five months. When she said she found someone, I was happy for her, congratulating her even. But she stopped all contact. There was no reason given. It vanished like a puff of smoke. It made me feel that lesbians can't have friends — or at least female friends. Probably something to do with jealousy or female rivalry, I don't know. But it hurt losing a friend simply because I became a third wheel. It wasn't the first time this happened to me either.

And with that, my lesbian days were over. I don't hate them. I never could. Being gay opened my eyes, gave me a different perspective on life. And yes, I was persecuted for merely looking at a woman. One guy passed and yelled out, 'Fucking lesbian.'

I admit the woman I was staring at was attractive, but that wasn't why I was looking at her. She seemed familiar and I was trying to remember where I saw her. He was gone before I could retort, 'It's better than being a fucking prick.' Probably for the best that I didn't. Gays get killed for less.

It is disgusting that homosexuals get beaten up, killed and persecuted for simply loving someone of the same gender. It's a shame really because some of them are nice people — well, the ones I spoke to in clubs were but unfortunately they had partners. Pity I could never find the nice single ones, although Maia was nice; I just couldn't give her what she needed.

I'd been ruined by the time Maia came into my life. I cannot fathom why those I met treated me the way they did. It left an emptiness in my soul that has never been refilled. And the reasons will remain an unsolvable mystery.

CHAPTER 6

I left my heart in Sheffield

Then there was Freya. Ah, Freya. Like a cool breeze on a soft, warm spring day; eyes that could melt your heart; a personality that stole your soul. She was my first true lesbian love. She was the only woman I made love to and kissed. She was my everything. And she destroyed me.

I met Freya through penpal writing. It started as brief communications before blooming into book-style letters. We were happy to report on everything we did, what happened to us, our experiences, ups and downs. We confided in each other for ten years. She was the first person I came out of the closet to, fearing I would lose her forever considering the animosity against homosexuals.

I am not sure if she reciprocated with the purpose of using me or abusing me, or if she truly was a lesbian. But she admitted as much to me as well. To say she used me, I don't really know. The lovemaking was unbelievable. I only wish I could have explored other methods with her. I never got the opportunity.

When we discovered we were both gay, our letters became more flirtatious and intimate. We would call each other and speak for hours. When we couldn't afford the phone calls, we would chat online, again for hours. I wouldn't get to bed until two in the morning. It was bliss and I truly believed I had found the one.

Freya lived in England. She was studying at the time I wrote her — what her subject was will remain a secret, to avoid identification. But in 2001 she graduated and took me totally by surprise.

'I'm going to come to Australia to see you.'

I was stumped. Yet my heart fluttered at the prospect to finally have her in my arms. Over the course of a few months, we arranged what we would do, places she wanted to see, places I could take her, and I worked out where I could provide the ultimate romantic rendezvous. However, I didn't want a one-off interaction, a visitation; I wanted a lifetime. It dawned on me very hard one day, waking up with the thought, 'I need her in my life, forever.'

A few weeks later, during one of our telephone conversations, I finally had the courage to slip in a question which I hoped didn't sound demanding. 'What would you say if, when you come to see me, I go back to England to be with you?'

She was all for it. I couldn't believe my luck. She loved me enough to want to be with me too. Either that or my mind assumed this was the case. It was like winning the lottery, at least I'm sure that would be a proper analogy. I've never won the lottery, well not the big one.

I said it before, I'll say it again; love makes you do stupid things. Is moving to a new country to be with someone, stupid? I knew her for ten years. We flirted and called each other for at least half a year before we met face to face, at least I think it was six months. I destroyed all her letters. No evidence left to confirm dates.

But one date I will never forget is 24 July 2001. Despite my father dying on this same day six years later, this date has embedded itself into my soul with a deadly grip. It refuses to let go. I'll see if I can paint the picture. It's a little fuzzy.

We were in her attic room in her Sheffield house. It was afternoon. She was sitting on her bed. I sat beside her. I looked deep into her eyes and smiled. She smiled back. I kissed her, passionately. I pushed her into the bed and began undressing her. I 'played' with her. She reciprocated. A vague memory of one of us on top of the other torments me. I enjoyed the time and I had fun. I only hope she did too. This was the last day I enjoyed a session of lovemaking. I never had another, ever again.

That's right. 24 July 2001 is the last day I ever had sex. (*'Can we just lose our virginities again? Because I think mine is growing back.' — Chandler Bing — Matthew Perry, love your work.*) I doubt priests have gone without it as long. Sorry, that was probably a little harsh. But sometimes I do use humour as a defence mechanism, especially when I am nervous. Give me a break, okay? This is very intimate stuff and not the kind of thing one should share willy-nilly. I'm sharing it because she was a big part of my life. She helped build opinions and feelings. She was an experience I needed to make me the person I am today.

Within a week of this encounter, she came up to me and said, 'We need to talk. It's not going to work out. It's not you, it's me.' (*Oh, the irony. Pluto flashback.*) Within a day, I was in a hotel crying my eyes out. She didn't even want to discuss it. 'Just, go.' It echoed — not word for word exactly — how I dumped my boyfriends. Karma is a real pain in the proverbial.

To this day, I have no idea what I did, if I had done anything at all. Perhaps the lovemaking wasn't as good as I thought it was. She never complained. Was I clingy again? We went out a couple of times but I'm sure I gave her the space she needed, and I visited tourist spots alone. Was she upset when she went to see a friend, and I didn't go? Maybe I needed my space as well. Would we still be together if I went with her to meet her friend? She didn't say anything about the fact they wanted to see me. Or perhaps holding her hand while we walked and me dropping it when I saw someone approach hurt her. I hated confrontation. I didn't want any excuse for someone to attack us. If it was a problem, she said nothing. (*And here's the need for mind-reading skills to be present. Where does one go to learn to do that?*)

Within a couple of days, I was in Scotland visiting one of my other penpals, Faunus — more about him later. And I think, if it wasn't for him, I probably would have resorted to something more violent against myself, again.

I stayed in England for four months. Tried to find work. The plan was to work in England and visit Europe as often as I could on weekends or annual leave. It never eventuated. I could only secure a temp job — ten weeks of it — but nothing permanent. Nothing else was forthcoming.

My cousin provided accommodation. Unfortunately, he also lived with his sister and her family — three kids included. For him to allow me to stay, made me see him as a true hero, but I think I overstayed my welcome, despite trying to find another place to live.

One day I simply got fed up with everything and decided to return home. His sister told me, 'Perhaps it's time you left.' That's how I knew I'd overstayed my welcome. I was hoping to be out of there before something like that happened, but it wasn't to be. And the day I planned to do something about arranging travel was 11 September. How was I to know terrorists would bring a halt to practically everything? I was uncertain I should be going anywhere. But I needed to; I wasn't welcome anymore.

My decision to leave England was a result of a constant message on the television, relentlessly saying, 'We need to stop these terrorists.' I agreed with it, but not as passionately as those speaking it. With every spoken word, I saw the target over England getting bigger and bigger. Despite one woman at my workplace explaining her experiences during the Cuban missile crisis, which brought a little strength to my soul, the relentless message was making my security vanish because I could feel a terrorist attack coming to London. A week after 11 September, I made the decision to leave. I was home by Guy Fawkes Night, 5 November 2001.

Dropping everything you know and to understand new rules, laws, customs, traditions, a way of life, is daunting. To do it for someone special seems like a great idea at the time, making you appear all heroic and full of sacrifice. But take it from me, it is the biggest mistake you can make, especially if the other party doesn't appreciate you or reciprocate your love.

Moving to England to be with Freya was the most sacrifice I made for anyone. I never committed such an act again. I never had the opportunity — well, almost one more with Larunda, but more on her later. Coming home, I was devastated. I could not fathom the idea of ever being happy again. I deliberately made sure nothing entered my life that would provide even an ounce of glee. I stopped listening to music. I stopped watching movies. I stopped writing stories. I gave up on practically everything. I was also unemployed, which slowly strangled my soul.

Love makes doing stupid things look like child's play. It's easy to make mistakes when you're in love. It blinds you; it misguides you; it violates your deepest morals. I am sure there are those that make it a success. But my life has been anything but successful. That might be a little harsh and untrue, but at the time, it was how I felt. Today? I look back on these memories without regret, merely sorrow. What would have happened if she hadn't kicked me out?

CHAPTER 7

Love finds a way to reach you again

Freya tore my heart from my chest and shredded it before my eyes. She put a fire to my soul and drenched it with a cold brew of betrayal. My life was over. Broken hearts are very difficult to mend, almost impossible when you're alone. I couldn't trust anyone, and I still don't trust people. While Freya started me along the distrust path, she wasn't the one who pulled it from underneath me, allowing me to fall into the cynical abyss. Many others came my way, forcing my mind to keep erecting barriers and locking iron doors with loud clangs.

The Freya year — 2001 — destroyed me. The devastation lasted seven years. Strange how it matched the misery I caused myself with that handsome artist. Despite the depression, I found a full-time job, I bought a property, I started living alone and I was trying to survive the pain and torture of what

Freya did to me. Several times I would cry myself to sleep. Many times, I couldn't sleep at all. My job was going from bad to worse and it began eating my sanity like a ravenous bug. My depression was accelerating faster than a falling piece of burning space debris.

Thinking things couldn't get any worse, my mind did another betraying act. Obviously fearing I was leading myself to suicide again, it repeated the imaginary friend/fantasy crap all over again. This time, it latched on to an English actor. Despite this guy's cuteness, after the shit I had to go through trying to get the musician out of my mind, I thought my brain would have learnt its lesson that this was not a good solution to fixing my problems.

I fantasised over Mr English Actor for about two years, much less than the original fantasy (*thank God*), before I had to find some way to stop myself drowning in another suffocating obsession. Don't forget, I pushed everything out of my life to stop happiness entering. To get this guy off my mind, I returned to writing. I should thank him for forcing me to do something proactive to get my life back on track, but it wasn't him; it was my mind. And there was this boy riding his bike to school every day when I went to work: a doppelganger for this actor. It was a challenge convincing my mind to drop him.

I wrote a story titled *STAI — Self Training Artificial Intelligence*. Okay, not a good title, but it was a start. It featured a woman who was abducted by aliens and experimented on by the insertion of a computer AI to half her body. She used it to escape. She met other aliens who were subjected to torture by the abductors and set about trying to help them. I put myself into the main character because I needed fantasy to focus my mind on something other than an obsession. (*Given she was torn in half, it mimicked my feelings.*) In essence, I was erecting a wall against the world. But the truth of the matter was, the story was a way for me to get over Freya.

It was a love triangle between my character, a female character representing Freya, and a male character who represented my sanity. Perhaps I did it as a way of trying to make sense with what she had done. It was written from the perspective of each character (*not a good start*) and probably not a good read, certainly not publishable, but my dad liked it. It was the only story of mine he read, which is a reason I will not amend it — I am sentimental. And yes, it had lesbian qualities. Maybe he knew what I was; I never got to tell him.

I think the lesson from the imaginary friend fantasies was about how to use my creative ability to get my life moving forward. But it had the risk of developing obsessions. These are dangerous. They stop life. You cannot move forward because you cannot think of anything other than the object of your desire. They drain your intelligence, they drain your energy, they drain your sanity. If that artist hadn't married, my life would have been much different. I would probably be in a mental ward, if not a coffin. And there would have been no reason why I would have met or fallen in love with Freya.

When my mind threw the English actor at me, I thought I was repeating history, but it forced me to wake up and, more importantly, grow up.

I have had a lot of bad years in my life, but none worse than 2007. It hit with the force of a supernova. And it happened to occur on the anniversary of my very last intimate session with someone. The idea of sex was nowhere near my mind at the time. I was in the ICU at a local hospital. My father had passed away from leukaemia. It was 4:30 am. As soon as we arrived home, mum went to bed, crying.

I couldn't sleep. How could I? My father had died. And in two hours I had to be at the airport to pick up my uncles and aunt who were flying in from Sydney. Who cares that I hadn't slept in twenty-four hours? My mind was obliterated into grief, worse than what Freya could achieve. It refused to let me rest. To pass the time, I wrote my father's eulogy, the one I spoke at the church through tears and sobs.

It wasn't a good year. I needed something to take my mind off the grief. My social life was empty, my love life non-existent and now I had lost a parent. Plus, I was still reeling from IR law changes introduced the year before which lost me a full-time job and allowed the company to steal a working day from me. This resulted in choosing between missing a mortgage payment or going three weeks without food. What kind of choice is that? Homelessness or death. Take your pick.

I ended up moving back in with the folks to survive and keep my property, despite it making me feel I was sacrificing my independence. Had to let mum know where I was going and when I would be home. And, like the good little courteous girl I am, I gave in rather than saying something like, 'I'll get home when I get home.'

Given dad's passing, I couldn't leave mum alone. She couldn't cope well, and I supported her where I could. I still live with her today, not because she needs me, but more importantly because I need her. I have no one else. And to top all the bad things, I had swapped jobs from loss adjusting to insurance brokering, which was a nightmarish hell even Satan couldn't replicate. Life wasn't great.

I needed a vice. I found it in theatre. There was a nice non-profit club that held 'cold read' auditions (*not good at auditions, reading off a script made it easier*), which I joined in 2008. It started a path into acting. It was off to a good start and life started turning around, if only a little. I wasn't looking for romantic partners, I wasn't looking for anything from anyone. All I needed was something to take my mind off my problems and acting was that solution. To say I fell in love with the theatre would probably be overkill, but I enjoyed it.

My mind could have easily given me another celebrity to fantasise about, but the second fantasy obsession fiasco taught me, 'You don't need to fantasise, you need to seek and do something.'

Within six months, theatre had given me the courage and confidence to find something else. What I sought was a partner, someone I could live my life with, someone I could love and be loved by, and someone who understood me. But I had new problems. I simply didn't trust people and I hated going out. I had grown into a home body. Even today I would rather stay home. The Covid-19 lockdowns didn't affect me. It takes a lot of energy to get the courage to step out the door for anything other than work or walking the dog.

I thought the best way to find someone was to go online. How bloody naïve was I? Do you know the dangers of that? Scams, fraud artists, men pretending to be women, arseholes, murderers — to name a few. But I found a lesbian dating site. It's where I met the teacher — who I think was first — and Larunda. We started as casual acquaintances and got to know each other.

Larunda lived in Victoria. She talked about her dogs. And she knew I liked muscle cars, often sending me pictures of V8s and other vehicles she thought would pique my interest.

And the day our friendship morphed into an intense relationship is a day not really celebrated for love; it's immortalised for sacrifice. It was Anzac Day, 2009. As it was a public holiday, we had nothing to do and we chatted online. I think we were there for about six hours, taking breaks to do what nature needs — food and the other thing. It was flirtatious, it was steamy, it was hot — and that's not describing the day itself. I had the AC on; it must have been hot outside.

By August, we agreed that she would make her way up to me and I would travel down to Victoria with her. Only for a holiday, I don't think it was going to be permanent. I had learnt my lesson from Freya, despite having potential to do the sacrifice again. But it scared the hell out of my mother. 'You don't know this woman.'

I'm like, 'Well, duh, that's why I want to do this. To really get to know her.'

Mum was worried this woman would be a killer or kidnapper. Mum often had paranoid thoughts like these and I think her way of thinking rubbed off on me over time. I think I'm too cautious for my own good.

The trip didn't proceed. It wasn't because of mum. It was because of me. Apparently, asking questions is not a good relationship builder. Larunda dumped me on 31 December 2009 because I was asking too many questions and she didn't want to start the new year with me.

I stared at her email for a while. I lost all manner of the concept of time. Galaxies could have formed and died before I snapped back into reality. Did I read it correctly? I got dumped simply because I asked questions? How the hell are you supposed to get to know people? Did I miss something? Was there a new technique for understanding people simply by looking in their eyes? Can you read minds? I can't. Did the world evolve into something different while I was in my depression years?

It threw me. Her new year might have started okay, mine exploded into oblivion — 2010 wasn't looking good. I really thought I had a shot at love with Larunda but obviously I missed the signals about not asking questions. Am I being ridiculous here? To this day I can still not understand this or why it happened.

CHAPTER 8

They always come in threes

By the time I met Verdandi, I was a wreck. I wanted love, then I didn't want it. I needed sex, but was disgusted with the prospect of it, not wanting to do it at all. I required a friend but thanks to my trust issues, didn't want to risk it. My mind lectured me that people don't know how to be friendly or caring without needing something in return. It messed me up bad, I'm surprised Verdandi stayed with me as long as she did.

I met Verdandi sometime in 2010. And the year she stopped caring was 2017. Seven years. They always come in threes. Wasted seven years on the gorgeous musician; wasted seven years after Freya shredded my heart and soul; and Verdandi lasted seven years. To say this was the longest relationship is wrong. It wasn't a relationship at all. It was a friendship. It could have been more, but she wasn't interested.

When I met her, she was emerging from an intense and abusive relationship with another woman. I think they were together for five years. She explained the incidents that drove them apart. Verdandi said because of her partner's violent nature, if she found us together, I could be in serious trouble. Verdandi was always on the lookout.

We started as friends because that's all she needed at the time. Me? I wanted more. (*Like Maia, only in reverse — irony is a bitch.*) I was patient. Hell, if my past relationships had taught me one thing, it was not to rush into anything. Within a year, however, my feelings were growing and getting stronger. I tried ignoring them because I couldn't detect any signal Verdandi was interested and I didn't want another heartache.

By December 2011 I couldn't hold my feelings back anymore. They demanded satisfaction. I needed to tell her how she made me feel and how I needed to be more than a friend. Fearing I would choke on my words in front of her — so much for courage and confidence — I wrote it all in a letter. About one page.

I sat there, watching her read my words of love and devotion. Her eyes welled, she smiled, and all looked positive. She put the letter on the table and stared at me.

'Thanks for those kind words, but I just got out of a difficult relationship and I'm not at that moment right now. Thanks, but no thanks.' Her words drove a stake in my heart.

I can see how what I did to men was being done to me — the guy after Janus went in for the kiss and I rejected him.

However, his was the first night. Mine was a year after I met the woman. Yet here I was, being rejected.

But I had to respect her wishes. Forcing someone to love you won't make it work. Love must flow equally and naturally for it to be the most beautiful thing ever. It might need a little nudge here and there, but you can't go in for the big L from the word go — at least I can't. How arranged marriages can work is beyond my imagination. How they do it, I can't even fathom. I know sparks can fly but this situation required patience. Obviously, a year wasn't long enough. And I knew that forcing Verdandi into a relationship would only be as toxic as the one she left. I agreed, apologised for making her feel uncomfortable — which she said I didn't — and I swallowed my pride.

We stayed friends. At least I can say pouring my heart out to her didn't push her away. We would go out and have lunch, or a coffee, or would hang out at her place or go to the movies. Saw *Prometheus* with her; walked out with a headache. It was the last movie I saw at the cinemas. She came to my place once. My dog didn't like her, barking at her and staying close to me. Dogs are a marvellous judge of character. I should have paid attention to my dog's reaction, but I was still in love with Verdandi at the time.

One fateful night, Wednesday 22 April 2015 to be exact, my emotions and all concept of life were destroyed. It happened during my theatre club's short season of one-act plays, right before the first performance. This was the last day

I felt love. My mum says everything bad seems to happen in April. Guess she was right. Although Larunda and I fell in love in April, giving weight it isn't all that bad.

The stage manager came out on the stage. She has a nice face and a wonderful personality. She never struck me as being a lesbian, but you can't judge a book by its cover.

But Verdandi suddenly went, 'Oooh, she's hot. What's her scene?' She faced me with a desperate plea in her eyes. 'Is she single?'

Verdandi wasn't interested in me but fell for this stage manager in a flash. She didn't even know the woman yet it seemed her loins melted to bursting point at a simple glance. What the hell? Did my heart explode? No, it didn't. It fell. It sank. It drowned in an abyss of pain and hurt. It tore apart as the crush depth squished it into nothing. I knew at that moment, Verdandi and I as a 'we' would never happen.

What the hell was wrong with me? Was I not hot enough? Was I not kind enough? Was I too clingy? Was I not clingy enough? Did I smell wrong? Look wrong? Breathed too much? What the hell was wrong with me?!

A very large part of me died that night. I lost love. I lost all ability to feel it, give it and lost belief in it. That night, she hurt me beyond what any words could describe. Romance was obliterated. To me, it was all a lie. True love, romance, intimacy — they didn't exist. They were myths like elves and dragons. They were figments of someone else's imagination. Love died that day. I never thought I'd find it again.

Despite the situation's claws, I remained friends with Verdandi afterwards, not with the hope of it ever blooming into something precious, but because I had no other friend in my life. I needed a social contact. I needed that connection. I needed some sense of belonging.

Even before she destroyed love, when we went out, she would always talk about her ex as if she was the only person in the world that really mattered. Considering the woman's violent nature, Verdandi would still see her. How crazy is that? Love certainly blinds you to sanity.

Out of nowhere, Verdandi found religion. She thought it was the best thing ever, like there was nothing else in the world important enough to talk about. Being born and raised a Catholic, I had done my time with Bible bashing. But every meeting we had, out came the religious stories.

I told her, 'I'm happy you found some solace in religion, but I've had my fair share of it and to be honest, I don't want to rehash it or return to it.'

She was appalled. I continued. 'The way I see it is this, there are too many religions in the world. Most say they are the definitive and true religion. To believe in others is a sin. To believe in all, is a sin. In the end you're damned if you do and your damned if you don't. I say, be damned and have fun.'

She had hurt me. Maybe I reciprocated. It wasn't my intention to hurt her, I wanted her to know my feelings about religion. It felt like she didn't respect me because the sermons would continue, and she had no care for my feelings. I even told her people avoided me because I wouldn't switch faiths. I guess this is what she did to me. Perhaps she was trying to recruit me and I simply shot her down. Did she see me as a soul in need of saving? My soul needed love. If I needed to be saved, I needed love, not religion.

Even when we accidentally bumped into each, she would remind me there were stories in the Bible that held truth. Whoever got his or her claws into her, certainly corrupted her. What religion does is blind you to other opportunities by teaching you there are no alternatives. (*Don't hate me for my opinions.*) But it wasn't her religious birth that killed the friendship. It was a luncheon.

We arranged to meet at a restaurant. By the time I arrived, she had already ordered her lunch and was sitting down. I stood in line to order mine, but she didn't join me. When I sat down, she spent a great deal of time on her phone. It was obvious she didn't want to be there. We hardly spoke a word.

Her lunch came before mine. I had to wait. When mine came, she had finished. She was eager to leave. She was distant. Her body was there but her mind was absent. It made the Trappist system look closer. (*For the record, the Trappist system is forty light years away. Gives you a perspective of where this friendship headed.*) After lunch, she went straight to a key cutting shop outside the restaurant, something about getting a car key recoded. As soon as she finished with them, she immediately grabbed her phone and called someone, staying on the phone for a long time. In all this, she didn't talk to me. I got fed up waiting, tapped her shoulder and indicated I had to go. She nodded and returned to her conversation. It left me feeling I had wasted an hour of my life.

Despite this treatment, I still needed a friend. Unfortunately, she was the only one I had. I wished someone else existed. I tried one last time to meet and have some company. I left messages on her phone. I tried three times. She never responded. And that was 2017. I didn't dump her. She dumped me — without words. It was all action. I prefer words. Hell, I would've even accepted, 'It's not you, it's me'. But her cold treatment made a blizzard in Antarctica in the dead of winter feel warm.

And with that, I lost all faith in being a lesbian. If this was how they behaved and treated others, I wanted nothing to do with it. The phase had burned and died. I had nothing left.

You can see how I had no interest in romance when I met Maia. The first stab was Verdandi's interest in the stage manager after I poured my heart out; the second her religious bashing; and the last, that luncheon disaster. After Verdandi, it was like, 'Why bother? Why should I date someone else? Why should I even consider bringing anyone into my life? What was the point of seeking company in the first place?'

Poor sweet, adorable Maia; she stood no chance.

My time in the sun had died. It had set into a constant darkness. The movie *Dark City* comes to mind. Romance, love and any interest in people, whether to be friend or more, died. I could never trust anyone again. They all possessed daggers with nuclear tips. Each had plunged their blades into my back, like a re-enactment of Caesar's assassination.

My first kiss made me sick. My first time with a guy deflated my ideals. My first time with a woman ended in a crushing blow. My last shot of love destroyed the very fabric of romance. And my first love was a figment of my imagination. Is there any wonder I reject the concept of a partnership?

CHAPTER 9

Life Choices

At birth, we are blank canvasses waiting for the world to paint a portrait of us. The brushstrokes come from parental guidance, school teachings and peer pressure. When the hormones kick in, they add colour in frenzied whacks and lashes.

Life is a journey of choices. Do I eat chicken or beef? Or not? Do I wear skirts or jeans? Do I love men or women? Everything comes at us like forks in the road. We must decide which path to take. And those choices are based on what we experience, what we feel at the time, and life in general.

Choosing to be gay was like the final piece of the puzzle had been correctly placed. But as my experiences revealed, the choice was not the right one for me. I choose *not* to be gay anymore.

Would I return to men? No, I don't think I can. I have no

love left in me, not for a human anyway. I have a dog. And at least I can get an unconditional love from her. She makes me feel appreciated and loved. And she's a perfect judge of character. She warned me about Verdandi. There was also another guy she hated, barking at him constantly, and he ended up committing sexual assault (*not to me*). To say love is completely dead in me is not correct. I have enough to give an animal. True, not the love I need, but I'll take whatever I can get.

I do see couples very much in love. They always appear to be having fun. Am I envious? No. My experiences have stymied me from ever contemplating a relationship. To be honest, I fear entering one because there is the lingering doubt it will end in a short period of time and do more damage. If I am crazy enough to risk a relationship and it ends, it will devastate me to the point I don't think even my fantasy-creating mind will be able to stop the knives entering my flesh. Besides, it's been a long time since I enjoyed intimacy, I fear I would not be able to perform adequately enough for the other person. It wouldn't be fair on them.

I never celebrated a first anniversary with anyone, other than my very first birthday, but hell, I have no memory of it. My longest relationships were eight months with Larunda and six months with Janus. I can't classify Freya as the longest because the first ten years we were simply friends with no indication that was where we were heading.

I live with my mother. She needs me and I need her. When

she passes, all I will have is my dog. I do have a sister, but her lifestyle is jammed packed she has no time left for me — more on her later. As for other family members, there is no direct contact with me. When mum says, someone 'said hello', I take her word for it because I'm not sure they said it. She at least likes to make me feel involved.

My choices led me to experiences that made me who I am, formulated my beliefs and helped create a fortress against the world. This is me. I am lonely and forever single. I refuse to let people in because I don't trust them. I never can. And I feel sorry for the person who wants to prove life is worth living because they will have to work very hard to prove themselves to me. They will most likely give up because it will be too difficult. And if they succeed? I suppose the reward would be beyond the moon.

Do I hate people? No. Hate is a powerful word. It results in the deaths of innocents. The disasters of 9/11 and Christchurch are examples. Religion seems to inspire hate. It might pretend to teach love and respect, but it blinds fanatics into thinking their religion is all that matters, and they get upset when people don't follow their faith and become angry when others challenge it. This leads to killing. We've been doing it for thousands of years. It will never change. (*I dare someone to prove me wrong.*)

I am not a hateful person. I have my phobias, but they are fears, not hate. And I can never hate anyone. Despise? Oh yes. I despise many. Paedophiles, terrorists of all faiths, politicians, greedy businesspeople, uncaring criminals, war-mongering arseholes, to name a few. There is a long list.

Do I despise my life? I certainly don't hate it. I don't trust people. I don't trust institutions. I don't trust myself when my mother passes. But despise? There are aspects of it I despise, like not being assertive enough to fight the bullies or telling the teachers not to attack me as well; poor choices in the relationship zone; wrong career path — although this last one has changed and given a ray of hope. More on this later.

As for regrets, the only ones I have are my suicide attempts. While they taught a valuable lesson, it makes me sick to think I would have taken my life due to the influence of others. When I die, it will be by Death's hand, not mine. I do not fear it. I will embrace death gracefully and accept its decision on my life if one could call this a life — living alone and constantly in fear is not living. *'Yea though I walk through the valley of the shadow of death, I will fear no evil…'* Death cannot do to me what everyone else has managed to do. Death will alleviate me of the pain.

CHAPTER 10

The forgotten experience

Holy cow! Juventas. She was a school friend from Fiji. How the hell could I forget her? I'm sorry that this is out of sequence, but it suddenly hit me.

Imagine this girl: red hair, fair skin, freckles on her face. I can't remember her eyes. Why can't I remember her eyes? They are the windows into someone's soul. Considering I was only nine or ten when I befriended her, soul searching had no meaning to me. Kids only want fun. At least I did.

She had all the hallmarks of a bully. She threw her cat over the balcony to see if it would land on its paws. It didn't. As I picked it up, it cuddled into me for safety. It swung out its paw and scratched her when she tried to take it from me. Juventas really wasn't a nice person. And she certainly ignored me in 1986. That's why Vesta became such a good friend because Juventas abandoned me. But in 1985? Juventas was my best friend. She treated me with respect. We even had sleepovers, despite my mother not remembering them at all.

'I would never have allowed it,' she said in disbelief. But the truth is, they happened. At least one of them in particular.

Details are scarce. We slept in the same room. I slept in her bed. We got naked and laid on each other. Hell, we were kids for heaven's sake. What the hell were we doing?? Did she instigate it? Did I? No, I don't think I would have. I had no concept of lying naked with anyone, sex was not taught to me. Where the hell was the parental supervision? Or perhaps her parents taught her this or she saw them doing it and wanted to check it out for herself. I have no idea.

Did her parents abuse her, and she thought it was normal to do that to someone else? Did she have any idea what she was doing, or was she having fun? Or perhaps it was the ultimate abuse, a higher level of bullying. And considering I forgot her until now, does it really matter? There is nothing I can do about it. I can't ask her anything. I don't even know where she is.

Was she my first lesbian experience? It appears to be, but we didn't kiss, we didn't do anything lesbians usually do. We simply laid there, naked. We were ten years old, for mercy's sake. What child knows the concept of sex? They never taught it to us in school in those days. Stranger danger wasn't bashed into us like a biblical mantra. It was a different time.

Is this where my lesbian ideals stem from? Not sure. By the time I realised I was attracted to women, I had already dated eight men. If I had lesbian tendencies, I would have been dating women from the start. Juventas was long forgotten; she didn't even appear as a footnote. I cannot blame her for my choice. Even if she instigated it all, in the end it was my choice.

What a revelation. Ten years old and I laid naked with a girl. Should I be charged for underage sex? Does it make me something I despise with a passion? All my adult experiences were over the age limit. Juventas was the only one who was ten. I was ten. What could this all mean? Surely it must be more than two kids experimenting with something they had no clue as to what it was or where it could lead. Not even sure if I could call it abuse. It didn't hurt. Her abandoning me hurt. Or did I leave her? Damn my failing memory. It's enough to screw the mind further into oblivion.

How could I forget this? Why did I forget this? The memories show me it wasn't traumatic. It was consenting. I agreed to it. Perchance all the bullying at the various schools bashed it deeper into my subconscious. I had to focus on today and forget the past. But it is the past that defines you, why forget it?

Looking at it with fresh, burnt-out eyes, with a love-lost soul, it was an encounter with no consequence. It only happened once; no other memories are forthcoming. And considering she abandoned me in 1986, maybe it was something she wanted to do and realised it wasn't right. Perhaps she couldn't face me for shame. Or she blamed me? Perhaps she was bullying me. Who knows?

Amazing when you look back at your past, you can really surprise yourself. Would I sue her for it? No, of course not. It was an event I've buried and long forgotten. It didn't influence my life in anyway — at least I don't think it did. It didn't sway my decisions — my experience with men did that. It was something time wiped from my memory, burying it under years of torture and dust. I have moved on.

CHAPTER 11

Even friends betray you

As I was getting used to the idea that I would never find love, never meet anyone to share my life and grow old with, I found another aspect where trust can be obliterated. Friends can be as cruel as lovers. And Faunus was the last of those 'friends'.

He lived in Scotland. He was the one I met after Freya kicked me out. I thank him for his support and assistance. He really was a sweet guy, but I had no intimate feelings towards him. Like Freya, our communication started with penpal letters. They grew longer and more involved.

After I returned home from England, we continued our communication. Somewhere along the line our letters began to get more intimate. We shared secrets, although I've forgotten his. Not even sure what I shared with him either. But it made us closer. Nothing like lovers though. Even 'friends with benefits' is going overboard. I could trust him, probably the last person I could do that with other than my mother.

In 2017, when Verdandi finally destroyed all hope of love for me, I got really drunk one night and connected with Faunus via Xbox online. The alcoholic stupor has stolen (*or buried*) the conversation, but apparently, as he told me later, I told him, 'I trust you with my life.'

What the hell? I did trust him, but not to that extent. To say something like that to someone is the ultimate trust-building statement. To allow your life to be in the hands of other people is an immense responsibility on their part and a great leap of faith on yours. You don't give your life to anyone unless they truly deserve it. It was a drunken mistake. I told him I didn't remember and apologised for it because it misled him, and it really wasn't true. I wasn't up to that level. Maybe at the time Faunus did deserve such a statement, but what he did next, proved otherwise.

He wanted to know where I lived. He had my postal address, not street address. I had his because he didn't have a box address. And he wanted mine. 'You have mine, why can't I have yours?'

He was demanding, insistent and persistent. Despite the fact I told him I don't trust easily, because I got drunk and uttered those words he thought I trusted him. Confusing to say I didn't. I did but not to the extent of letting him know exactly where I lived.

Over the course of a few weeks, I contemplated giving it to him. Why not? He was planning to visit Australia at one stage and he would come visiting, and I was starting to trust him more and more. But he destroyed everything, having the tenacity to tell me, 'I spoke to my friend in the US about you and she thinks you're crazy.'

If he wanted me to trust him, why did he speak about me to someone else? How does that build trust? It doesn't. And why should I care what some stranger really thinks about me? I didn't care. But him speaking about me behind my back hurt. You don't build trust by betraying it. What else did he tell her? Were all my secrets shared around like herpes? How was I to know?

You might think I am being silly here, but remember I was bullied practically every single day of my life. My romances — if they could be classified as such — fell flat and ripped my emotions like flaying flesh with a hot poker. And the more I shared, the less I received. Trust did not exist. To a bullied mind, it builds barriers and cautions you to everything around you. Safety, not only physical but also mental, becomes your main priority. Sharing details about your life and your identity becomes harder.

I am sure I told Faunus how my trust in people had been obliterated and, even though I trusted him, it wasn't at the level I apparently said it was — never trust alcohol. And yet, he was still insistent on getting my street address. He didn't give a reason, only that he wanted it. If he was truly a friend, he would have let the matter go. Therefore, I felt he wasn't a friend.

I had Facebook at the time. Yes, he was in my friends list. I put on my wall a call for help. I didn't mention names. I simply told people, 'I have this friend who is insistent on getting my street address and he won't take no for an answer. He knows I don't trust easily. What can I do?'

Some people responded. I've forgotten what they said. But his response via email hammered itself deep within my brain, it will never be dislodged.

'I saw what you said on Facebook and I don't appreciate it. Keep your fucking mouth shut.'

I barked back as hard, called him on the distrust. 'It's okay for you to talk about me to someone in the US but I can't talk to my friends about you? That's a little unfair. How can I trust you when you do something like that?'

He threatened me. 'If you leave me, I will kill myself.'

I didn't want him to do that. Death is not an answer. I learnt that at least. I went to Facebook again and told them what he had said. And of all the people to respond, it was Janus.

'That's emotional blackmail, sweetie. Dump the guy.'

Nice to know Janus still cared. I didn't want to let Faunus go as he was my last friend. In the end, I had no choice but to do what was advised, to protect my mental health. I dropped Faunus like a sack of bricks. And with that, my trust in people vanished like dust on the wind. All I wanted was a friend. All I got was a dagger in the back.

After this incident, no one kept in touch via Facebook. There is a saying, 'If you haven't used it in a year, get rid of it.'

It was two years afterwards that I set out to test my so-called friends on Facebook, as I explained previously. Friends! What a joke. You have connections, not friends. They don't meet you face to face. They don't visit you. You don't go out and meet them daily or weekly or even yearly; at least mine never did, and most were local.

Even friends betray you. It seemed every one of mine did. From my work colleague who introduced me to that drug dealer, to another friend who only used me for driving lessons. And I wasn't even insured to let her drive my car. She nearly involved us in an accident. As for the former, here's how she hurt me.

When I found out the guy did drugs, I told her. She was disgusted. She said she would speak to him. Apparently, she knew the problem having dealt with it before. But, when I tried to invite her out for coffee, she gave the excuse, 'I'm too busy this weekend, I'll call you next weekend.'

Naturally, she didn't call. I would call and try again on no less than three occasions. Her final response was, 'I'm too busy with my other friends.' Obviously I wasn't important enough for her.

Met up with her about six years later. She bumped into me at the shops. I think she wanted to let me know she was married because she introduced me to her husband. Told her my own news; I was living on my own. She appeared pleased.

She took my number and said she would call me. I'm still waiting for that call and it's been more than fifteen years.

In my final years of insurance, which would have been another six years from that shop meeting, she got in touch again, this time through email.

'Not sure this is the Teri I knew, but it is me, Nona *(fake name)*. Was hoping to reconnect.'

I was in desperate need of friends *(theme of my life)*. Naturally, I accepted her offer. We met at a restaurant for her birthday. I gave her a snow globe because I knew she loved them. It's the little details that show people how much you appreciate them. But it was all over as soon as it started.

About a month later, I sent her a message to see if she wanted to get together for coffee. No response. Tried again. Ditto. And on the third time I received, yet again, nothing. What else was I to do? I emailed her:

You wanted to reignite this friendship and you are ignoring me. I don't think that's fair.

She responded saying she had recently miscarried. Poor girl, but she never even told me she was pregnant. How the hell was I supposed to know? The world really must have developed psychic abilities and alienated me from the lessons.

My email was harsh, but I had been mistreated for many years, abused, bullied, harassed — not only with lovers and friends, but also at work — I reached a point where I had to speak my mind. I had no friends, I had no love, I had nothing left to give. It made me angry and I had wasted the last embers of my energy in fighting becoming bitter. I lost the battle. When she ignored me she received a full-frontal attack.

And what is worse, I didn't care. If she ever gets in touch I'm not going to give her the satisfaction of insulting me again. Once bitten, twice shy. But for her it is twice bitten. Shame on me.

Lastly, there was this guy ...

What you need to know about Vulcan is he was half my age. Won't say where I met him or how our friendship started — most likely will identify him — and given how it ended, a lot of people committed what he did; it could be any one of them, who will know? What connected us was a day I saw him and he looked angry. I asked if he was okay. He said he felt bullied. Given my experience, I tried to advise him not to give into the anger or give them the satisfaction of inflicting pain. It seemed to work.

Bullying was our connection. It was something we shared in common. Speaking with him I discovered other things we liked such as tennis, billiards — not that I can play well mind you — coffee. These were the interests that bound our friendship.

I never had any intention of dating him. I was satisfied having him as a friend. We would go out and enjoy lunches, play sport — and boy oh boy, was he competitive. Never won a game against him. I had to fight for every point in tennis.

One day, when we were having a coffee, he saw this woman. She was very attractive. I hate using the term 'out of his league' but I believe he thought it. Nonetheless, I encouraged him.

'Go say hello.'

He looked away, shyly. 'Are you kidding? What the hell would I say?'

'Hi, my name is Vulcan. How are you?' I started. 'That's not difficult, is it? You have to start somewhere.' Even I could have done that, but I simply wasn't interested. Love was already fading from my soul. He didn't even try.

But one day he hurt me. He came to my house and we stayed outside talking. He spoke about a woman he was in love with and unsure how to approach her. Think I gave him some advice. But he said, 'I can't talk to her like I talk to you. I like you, but not like that. I can't even think of doing *it* with you.' He gave a shiver as if the very thought of being intimate with me made him physically sick. Seriously, his entire body shook. Was I really that ugly?

While I never wanted to do that with him either, it was his reaction that hurt. A simple little rejection by words is bad enough. To see the action, it dug deep. I didn't cry. I didn't shudder. I didn't tell him off. I had no intention to be with him anyway, but he could have been a bit more diplomatic.

Did everyone see me like he did? Like a disease needing to be purged? Would that explain why women weren't interested in me? How could I alter their perceptions? It wasn't a nice feeling.

Unfortunately, he committed a sexual assault against a woman twice his age. I was appalled. He spent a few years in jail for it. I never heard from him again. Not sure I would want to, considering the type of crime. If he's capable of that, I wouldn't feel safe around him. Paranoia might be dictating this feeling considering he shuddered at the thought of doing *it* with me, but should I take the chance? That is something a woman should never have to experience. (*Perhaps I should feel blessed he thought me too ugly to consider having sex with, but it still doesn't make me feel good about him*).

My friendship acquaintances turned out to be a bust like my romantic interactions. It appeared fate was dictating to me that I must live alone. I cannot have lovers, I cannot have friends, perhaps I cannot even have life. But even death avoids me these days.

CHAPTER 12

Death used to be my friend

There have been six incidents in my life where death visited me. The first two exist only as stories mum told. I was eighteen months old when I contracted meningitis. I was in a coma for two weeks. The doctors didn't expect me to live. Yet here I am forty-seven years later and divulging intimate things. The other, I was badly food poisoned in Germany when we vacationed there in 1980. I had my fifth birthday in Florence, Italy. We left and a week later a massive earthquake hit the area. Was Death aiming for me there, but missed? He certainly caught up with us in Germany. Even mum and dad got sick.

By age ten, Death tried again. I was on school camp. There was a storm outside and trying to sleep was close to impossible. With perfect timing, I happened to glance out the window in my zillionth attempt to get comfortable when a bolt of lightning struck. The hole it created missed my window by three metres. We could stand in it knee-deep. The boom was deafening. The light searing. And I couldn't hear or see for five minutes afterwards. To a ten-year-old, it was scary. It felt like Death wrapped his claws around my soul and squeezed hard. I was even joked at, kids laughing at me because I was crying and they thought it was due to being scared of the storm. It wasn't the storm that made me cry; it was the fact I thought I was both deaf and blind at the same time. I only heard their jokes and saw them laughing when my senses returned.

Age thirteen saw my suicide attempts. Already spoken of them. And by age twenty-five, Freya destroyed me. While Death didn't visit, I wish he had because it felt like a near-death experience to me. I could certainly have died. A part of me did. I think both Faunus and my cousin stopped any suicide thoughts by simply being there. Looking back, it wouldn't have been that hard to kill myself. There were many places in England where I could simply disappear.

Another near miss happened when I was eighteen. I was driving to university and stopped at a red light. There was a BMW beside me, waiting patiently (*nice car*). The cross traffic stopped flowing and the lights began to change. When our green arrow appeared, I released the brakes and slowly moved forward. The hairs on the back of my neck stiffened as if an electric hand brushed them up. I slammed the brakes, not knowing why. The BMW stopped because I did. Suddenly this crazy streak of white zoomed past us, doing at least eighty in a sixty zone, coming from our right and moving to our left. Had we inched a few centimetres forward, the idiot would have slammed into me, shoved me into the BMW, and I might not have survived the impact. Yet, more was to come.

Within the next three kilometres from that set of lights, I was nearly run off the road three times by unforgiving 4WDs changing lanes erratically. I was a nervous wreck by the time I got to university. I don't think I absorbed much information that day. It was like Death was really trying to take my life and missing with each attempt. Practically bullying me. Either that, or my guardian angel stepped in. Wish he would involve himself in my love life as I've struck out.

When I turned thirty a power pole outside the office fell into the street with a loud crash. If it had fallen towards the office, it would have hit me or at least caused serious harm when it crashed into the building. I was in direct line with it. Perhaps Death was drunk when he chopped the wood via use of termites, giving them the wrong instructions and they chewed in the wrong direction. Scared the hell out of me and could have been a disaster if it hadn't fallen away from the building.

By age thirty-two, Death had stopped visiting. Or perhaps, he chose my father instead. Death was a part of my life, not in the conventional sense. But after I lost love in 2017, I could certainly have used his help, as a friend of course, or as a talking buddy. Knowing him, he would have given me the scythe, and not as a gift either (*my name is not Mort*). I probably would have accepted the cut, but mum needed my help.

It doesn't bode well for one's mental health when everyone rejects you, Death included. By God, what the hell is wrong with me? Thing is, given my experiences, it isn't about not letting anyone in; it's about self-preservation. If I got involved with someone, despite them having to work hard to break my barriers and get me to trust them, the fear it would fall apart like all the others would ultimately win over. Honestly, I would love someone to prove me wrong.

Despite me trying to kill myself all those years ago, I don't want to die. I may not like my life, I may not like life in general, but I can still see hope, promise and a future, even if it is a little dim. There is always hope. Love? Comes and goes, but hope remains.

Do I hate my lovers? No. I loved them. I cannot bring myself to hate someone I loved. I may not love them anymore, but it doesn't mean I hate them. They were the experiences I needed to help understand who I am, what I am and what I want.

I don't want Death. I want a friend. I want someone who appreciates me with no strings attached. You don't need to buy gifts to show appreciation. You need words. Kind, heartfelt words. You need connection, socialisation. You need communication. And yes, you need trust. But thanks to my experiences, I no longer trust, therefore I will not be searching for the one who can appreciate me. But I still hope they are out there, somewhere.

CHAPTER 13

Lack of engagement

Joining theatre in 2008 was one of the best decisions I made at the time. It was fun. And since writing my own plays and directing them, I've really enjoyed myself. While the people were friendly, for the most part, I thought I would have scored a decent friend or two out of it. You know the type, the ones who like your company enough to invite you places and do something with you outside of theatre. Unfortunately for me, I only have acquaintances and I only see them at theatre events.

Okay, I am sure any of them reading this will be getting upset, crying out, 'We are friends.' And I am sorry for being blunt, but a friend to me is someone who enjoys going out to have coffees, lunches, dinners, and doing something other than rehearsals, performances and seeing shows. Yes, we have Christmas functions, but that's only once a year.

And I don't get invites for them anymore because I'm not on Facebook.

We did have a small gathering of ladies dining out with the intention that someone at the party would be selected to conduct the next party. I only attended one. Not sure what happened there, but it stopped. If it is still going, I have not been invited.

And since the club moved to Facebook, they no longer use email to send invites. Everything is done through Facebook. It makes me feel alienated, especially when everything was done via email at one stage and they no longer do it. I won't return to Facebook either. My time on that social platform is done. And I feel freer without it.

What about me asking people out? Okay, let's open this door. As you have read, my experiences have driven me into a dark place. I cannot trust people. The mere thought of having to ask someone out stands my hair on end and the anxiety causes difficulty breathing. I break out in a sweat. In the end, I am so uncomfortable it would be useless going out.

To say I was unappreciated in the theatre, is a lie. They do appreciate me. At least they did. They do talk to me, most of the time, but only if I speak to them first. There are those groups that keep to themselves and, even saying 'hello' can make them look at you with glazed eyes making it seem as if they are wondering, 'Where the hell did you crawl out from?' They may be actors, but eyes never lie. There were those who snapped at me because they didn't understand the word 'patience' or had none for me. Some simply had no consideration for my feelings. Even though these cranky people were the minority, it was enough to destroy the love of theatre, or at least make me feel I was a fish out of water. I quit the theatre in 2022 because their attitudes brought all the suicide thoughts back, and I didn't need that in my life.

Throughout the fourteen years of theatre I enjoyed, I found I didn't have much to say. When at rehearsals, people often chatted among themselves, being social, but not including me. All I wanted to do was get down to business and go home. Often, I found if I didn't have a script in hand, I couldn't talk to people. Was this why they avoided me like the plague? It didn't really matter because I could never bring myself to engage.

One of the things that has trained my mind to isolate is how people have spoken to me in the past. They do all the talking. When I wanted to say my piece, they cut me off — friends, work colleagues, lovers, they were all guilty. Even mum does it sometimes. Don't think she realises it though. I could be talking when someone enters the conversation and cuts me off. When I try to speak, they keep talking, speaking over my voice and don't listen to what I am trying to say. They don't give me a chance to speak. To say it is rude is an understatement. It's downright inhumane. Whatever happened to civilised conversations?

Over the years I taught myself to simply shut up. If after the second attempt to speak I don't get my chance, I don't bother.

I silenced my voice. And, because of it, I don't speak much these days, if at all — other than to my mother — which is weird because as a child my nickname was Chatterbox. It's possible I said all I needed to say all those years ago. Or maybe love took my vocal cords when it abandoned ship.

As for gatherings, the only parties I attend are those my sister invites me to and even these are very selective. These days, all the invites come from mum; I don't get personal invites. It hurts that I have to be invited like a 'third wheel'. When I go to the parties, I find myself a corner or secluded spot and sit in it. I don't move. I don't engage — because I simply don't know how — unless someone talks to me, I'll be happy to oblige a conversation. But most of the time, I'm alone, quiet and bored. At the last party I attended my sister never engaged with me other than to say 'Hello' at the very beginning. It's why I don't go to them often because I suffer the same thing over and over. Lack of engagement is not shyness; it's a lack of trust the other person will let me speak or even listen.

My sister is a lovely woman who has a wonderful life. She is happy. And I am pleased she is enjoying life. We used to play tennis every Saturday morning for a few years. This had to stop when she began studying for her career. When she graduated it never resumed, but she does play tennis with other friends. Perhaps she finds my company boring. Don't see how as I used to make her laugh a lot. But it hurts she no longer involves me with her life. But I never complain. Who am I to dictate who she sees and what she does?

However, in 2019, it came to a point I had no choice but to make a stand. And after this event, I chose to disengage with any invite she sent to mum because of how she made me feel. It was my birthday. The day I came into the world all those years ago. Birthdays are supposed to be joyous occasions, a celebration, an event to share with family and friends. As I had no friends — only acquaintances who had nothing to do with me outside of theatre — the only ones I could enjoy the day with was family.

I invited her to have lunch with mum and me. She found it far more important to race her car than enjoy an hour with me on my special day. One basic little hour. That's all I was asking for and she couldn't even sacrifice time out of her day to do that. She may have booked the course in advance, but surely she could have known the date and say, 'Ah, that's my sister's birthday. She's bound to invite me to lunch like she did last year.'

I'm obviously asking too much consideration from people. Or maybe she believed I would be sacrificing enough to say, 'No problem, go ahead and enjoy yourself while I sit here all alone, by myself, with no one around to enjoy my special day.' I'm always sacrificing my happiness for others. Well, that year, I had enough. I expected a little sacrifice to come my way. I felt I deserved it, considering the rotten luck I had with social connections, unemployment, silence and everything else. This was me standing up for myself, my rights, my sanity; my one shot at selfishness and it backfired spectacularly.

When she refused and gave the reason, my whole body went numb. Not from shock; from pain. Such immense pain. I expected this type of treatment from friends, but from family? How did it make me feel? Irrelevant, meaningless, insignificant, estranged, unimportant, disliked, forgotten, abandoned, alienated, ignored, unloved, shunned, unvalued, unappreciated ... all of the above. Obviously, I'm not special enough to have people celebrate the day of my birth. And I certainly didn't feel special when she uttered her excuse. As a result, I no longer celebrate it. It's simply another day, another cog in the year to wake up, do work, eat and go to sleep. Nothing special, nothing gained, nothing lost other than time itself.

Why did it affect me? Simple. In 2019 I became unemployed for the second time in my brief existence. Unemployment strips you bare of all human essentials — like the will to live. Everyone who has told me they suffered unemployment have no idea how bad it really is because they often found work within three months. I was unemployed for the entire year, only scoring three interviews in 365 days with not one job in sight. I lost count of the applications I sent — at least five hundred — and out of those only about ten per cent would reply with an automated 'unsuccessful' response. There was no human to human contact. Humiliation did not express how it made me feel. I didn't even feel human. And when my sister shunned my birthday, it solidified society's inhumanity. I couldn't stand the pain and had to do something.

Considering all the negative reinforcement I received at school when trying to stand up for myself, how do you think this confrontation went? What do you think my chances were at success? Can you guess the result?

When I confronted her — via email mind you; getting time to see her face to face was impossible as she is always 'too busy' — and told her my feelings caused by her missing time with me on my special day, her response was, 'That's the way it is.'

In that one sentence I saw any and all opportunities to engage with my sister as unfeasible. She would not make time for me, she would not engage, and she would not budge on her decision, no matter what I said or how it made me feel. In that one sentence, I gave up on her.

Don't get me wrong, I still love my sister. I have to force myself to disengage from her because all she will do is hurt me again. I am happy she is enjoying life, really I am, but I have to accept the fact I will not be a part of it and she will not be part of mine either. All it means is I move forward with one less person in my life. Death does the same thing. Given all the friends I have had to cut out of my life, I'm used to cutting the cord of connections. But I never thought I would have to do it to family.

However, this one event — a non-event some people might say — destroyed all desire in me to engage with people or do something outside of my routine. That, together with being unemployed along with all the silence from the myriad job applications I kept sending, certainly made me feel worthless. I switched off my ability to participate in society and learnt to live with no one but my mother around me. I don't go out, not even to get out of the house. Well, that's not entirely correct. I walk the dog, but we don't go far, only around the block; her and me. No one else.

Would I reactivate it? Good question. Why should I? If people showed no interest in me, either via conversation or engagement, why should I bother? I have adapted to what life has thrown at me. I have found comfort being quiet and alone with my solitude. I don't have to worry about anyone, and I don't have to depend on anyone. There is a bliss in that, one I have wrapped around me like a blanket. I may be lonely, but I have a happiness no one else will understand. They can't hurt me here.

CHAPTER 14

No escape from them

To think my romantic life — if one can call it that — was the only form of abuse I received would be an utter lie. It's not like I didn't try to involve myself with people, either as a friend or something more, I did. I have shown you I did.

But I think one of the other reasons why trust is hard to come by these days has a lot to do with my working life as well. Like school, I received flak from both sides — customers and colleagues.

While the abuse, harassment and bullying were not constant, they were there enough to make life hell. We all have bad days, but some days were so beyond terrible that my mind would wave little insults of its own, throwing them like fists — 'you haven't thought of suicide in a while, isn't it time you did?'

Thankfully, my experience at age thirteen taught me that there is no problem too big that can only be solved by killing oneself. Naturally, I ignored my bad thoughts, but the pain of abuse still lingered. 'Abuse' is probably the wrong word because it implies that I was beaten up or physically assaulted in some way. Harassment is not strong enough a word. Bullying? Yes, it was a technique related to that, but even that doesn't convey what they did to me.

While I could list every single event here — if I could remember them all — I don't exactly want to bore you with too many and don't want this story to be simply a complaint about my life. I am trying to show how my life has not been pleasant and why I have chosen the solitary life. Despite my choice, I still try to bring people inside. But more often than not I am met with nuclear-tipped daggers in the back.

I have worked at various places over the course of thirty-two years. I started at a fast-food joint. Some people I met laughed at this. I don't know why. It's a job. It's a relatively good job for teenagers starting out in the working world. And today their pay is a lot more than I received — $3.50 an hour. Mind you, that was back in 1990. Besides, I firmly believe that about eighty per cent of the population has at one time in their lives asked, 'Do you want fries with that?'

There were two events that stick out at this job. First, a manager. I think she must have been a lesbian because her idea of personal space meant pushing herself on to my back. Once I had to clean out the coffee pot. Luckily it wasn't scolding, but I turned quickly and deliberately spilt it on her. It forced her to keep her distance from me, but her attitude turned a little nasty afterwards. She would constantly tease me. If this was her idea of turning me on, or sparking some admiration her way, she was sorely mistaken.

The other incident was regarding hours of work. I informed my manager I'd applied for another job because they weren't giving me the hours I needed or expected and advised that I could no longer work on Sundays. What did they do? They rostered me on Sundays and told me I had to choose between the jobs. Considering the second job paid $4 an hour more, I said goodbye. Guess it backfired for them.

The next position was at a service station. My roster started with twenty hours over the weekend, which suddenly turned to ten hours at some point. I did the shift leading up to the graveyard shift, finishing at 11 pm, with the last hour being totally on my own. It was okay. Saw me through university. Management and the team were good to work with, at least no bad attitudes spring to mind. Either there were none, or they have been suppressed. I did three years with them, how bad could it have been? The reason I left was security, or lack thereof. All I had was a wooden stick under the bench. After they found a balaclava in the bushes, my sense of security evaporated like the mpemba effect — boiling water thrown into freezing air creates a cloud of ice. Videos show it more like a cloud which disappears quickly.

I shifted to the bakery after this, working the afternoon

and evening shifts. This was where I met Nona. There are too many events here to list but there are two that stick out like a sore thumb.

The first started with my helper — management said she was my assistant. Instead of helping me clean the bakery and readying it for the next shift, she decided it was her prerogative to assist the deli girl to prepare the deli department for the next shift. That was not her job, it was not her responsibility, and she had no authority to do it. She was employed to help me.

On one shift I left the floor for her to sweep and empty one bin. I did everything else. When it was time to leave, I was dressed ready to go and she called me over the PA system. When I came out, she demanded to know why I left the bakery in the state it was in. I simply said, 'That's your job. I did everything else. You are, after all, meant to help me.'

It may have been mean of me to say what I did, but given she never helped me at all, despite me being nice to her throughout our entire working relationship (*well, at least up to that point*), I had started developing this Phoebe of *Friends* fame attitude; simply put, 'I don't give a tiny little rat's arse.' It was a form of standing up for myself and my rights which unfortunately backfired yet again, because the next day the manager demanded to know why I didn't clean the bakery the night before. I didn't lie. I simply said, 'Well, she was too busy helping little miss deli girl to finish doing her duties here.'

'Why was she in there? That isn't her place,' he said.

'Ask her. I didn't send her there.'

Did it fix the situation? Not really. He obviously spoke to her about responsibilities because every night she kept asking, 'Is it okay if I help in the deli?'

I couldn't be bothered telling the management about her lack of a work ethic because she possessed all the attitude and behaviour of, 'I'll do what I God-damn like, thank you very much.' Instead, I told her to finish her bakery tasks before helping in the deli. Not to say she finished all her tasks mind you, but I felt mentally better without her around me.

There was the girl who waited until I swept up the rubbish on the floor into a dustpan and lifted it to put it into the bin. She waited until the moment I placed the dustpan close to the bin before wrapping the bag and pulling it out, with dirt remaining in the dustpan. I asked kindly, 'Can you open it please so I can empty this?' She glared at me, smiled callously and said, 'No.' And no, she wasn't pranking. She meant what she said, taking the rubbish out of the bakery and leaving me with a dustpan full of dirt. I called her a bitch and got into trouble because she reported me.

Labelling her bitch was wrong, but she deserved it. Once again I explained the situation to the manager. Nothing was done. She still treated me poorly. All I ever did to her was smile and say hello.

I left the bakery to go to England — you know how that turned out. Upon my return, after about eight months on the dole (*or Newstart it was called*), I found a job in insurance doing reception work at a loss adjuster's office.

Everything was going peachy until we got a new assessor. He became the boss. At first, things worked smoothly. When Cyclone Larry hit North Queensland, it felt like the storm struck our office personally. We got about three hundred claims in a week. For context, we would usually only get twenty to thirty new claims a week. There were only two assessors and me. They didn't touch the claims until I set them up in the system, along with all the manual paperwork required. Luckily it wasn't my responsibility to arrange inspections; it was theirs. Due to the numbers received, I found I was taking work home and not getting paid for it despite already being underpaid at this job. Loyalty amounts to nothing these days.

A cyclone victim who lost part of his roof — didn't care his neighbour had no roof at all — demanded to know why, after two months, his roof was not repaired. He lived in Ingham, which is little more than an hour's drive north of Townsville (*if you stick to the speed limit*). After looking at his file, I saw the big fat roof repair authority sitting on the system. Instead of being pleasant about the matter, he bit my ear off. I don't want to remember the words he used, they have been deliberately suppressed, but I got the gist that Cyclone Larry was all my fault.

There you have it, folks. I have the power to conjure up cyclones. I am Mother Nature. Hell, if I had that power, I think a volcano would suit him swell.

I had to phone the repairer to find out a reason and call the client back with the answer. The delay was caused by a little-known phenomenon after cyclones called rain. Repairers don't get up on roofs in the rain. It's dangerous. Ingham received constant rain for a long time after the event. One or two days were spared, but the majority were constant tears from heaven. Repairers didn't have one house to repair, there were hundreds. Like I said, in one week we got three hundred claims. And that was only our office.

And when I thought the only harassment I would receive during working life was from customers, the new boss erupted like Mount Vesuvius. Krakatoa more like it.

By the time this happened, I was stuck doing first reports only. He had hired two more hands to deal with follow-up procedures and closing the files. He advanced one of them to an assessor rank without asking me if I would be interested in the position. I'd been working there longer. I probably wouldn't have done it anyway as insurance had already become a slowly twisting samurai sword in the gut.

With the first reports, I had to listen to the assessors on tape as they dictated what they wanted written. Nothing wrong with this per se, except they often dictated while they were driving. I had to contend with radios, engine noise, traffic noise, wind noise if they had their windows down, and static from their poor-quality devices.

Second problem with this was the length of the reports. Domestic and vehicle insurance claims were usually three to five pages long. Nothing too fancy. Unfortunately, the first

Chapter 14 No escape from them

assessor who worked these claims would hand me anywhere between seven to fifteen reports to do at once. It was time consuming. To add more salt to an already open wound, business and liability claims could be up to fifteen pages. And the second assessor, and boss, would dictate these claims. Sometimes he would give me one at a time, other times a whole bunch.

I always learnt to prioritise my workload. First in, first served. And since he started working with us, this wasn't a problem. Unless a report was urgent and they told me it had to be squeezed in before all others, the workload moved smoothly and without a hitch.

Until this horrible day. I was two reports away from finishing the first assessor's work when the boss stormed in wanting to know where his liability report was from the day before. He had never said it was urgent. I guess he expected me to either know or suddenly conjure up the ability to read his mind. He was upset and started yelling at me. Seriously, spray flew off his lips like a rabid dog.

He dragged the other assessor into the fray, screaming, 'My reports take precedence, you got that.' He turned to me with a menacing glare, yelling, 'Do you want me to fire you because you're not doing your job? Because I can do it.'

He said more threatening words before storming off. I wouldn't have minded being fired — severance pay and all — and I could certainly have sued them for unfair dismissal because I was in fact doing my job. But at the time I couldn't afford to lose it because I had a mortgage and I was on a single, underpaid wage. Adding to the insult, the government changed the industrial relations rules, allowing this company to give me the choice of losing my home or starving to death, as mentioned earlier.

After the abuse he sprayed at me I had to leave the office and go to the toilet to wash out my tears. Not that he cared. One of the other women came in and asked if I was okay. How can you answer a question like that after being berated by your boss? I felt worse than shit under a shoe. I didn't even feel human. I felt that whatever term I was supposed to be labelled with had yet to be discovered and I was nothing. In an effort to comfort me I believe, she told me that he had lost a friend that morning.

Instead of comfort, it rammed home the point I was nothing more than the boxing bag for his grief. Does that justify his behaviour? No, it doesn't. And it didn't reassure me. The only relief I got was after I left the job and I sued them for underpaid wages. Scored $6,000 out of them.

Unfortunately, the job I moved to was still in insurance. Brokering this time. At first, I didn't handle claims as they had an officer do that. When she left, they replaced her with a family friend, whom I believe suffered with depression. At least, that's what they told me, as if instructing me to, 'Please be nice to her.' I wanted to tell them to ask her to, 'step in line'. Depression was the story of my life. But I don't think they cared.

There were two other events that helped force me further into my shell and stop trusting people. And they happened at the same time. Thinking back, the second was more of a symptom of the first.

The first was when they expanded the office. It became an L-shaped environment. However, when they connected the air-conditioning to the new area, they didn't include a generator or whatever they use to cool air as it flows down the line. Consequently, the air in the new area was at least six degrees hotter than the rest of the office. To fix this problem, they adjusted the thermostat in the main area — where I was located — to eighteen degrees, providing them with their optimal twenty-four degrees. But even that was a little too hot for them. Sometimes it was set to sixteen degrees.

When it got too cold for me, I simply adjusted the thermostat to twenty-four again. This kind of worked until a sign was stuck on the device stating, DO NOT ADJUST THIS GAUGE!!!! Yes, in capital letters. Yes, with many exclamation marks. And yes, with no consideration for others.

I have bad blood circulation. What this means is, my extremities don't warm quickly. When I am cold, my feet and hands freeze as if I had plunged them into Antarctic ice. And they sweat at the same time. Because of this, the rest of my body quickly cools and doesn't warm fast enough.

To add to the problems, the office toilet was out in the common public hallway, which I don't think had proper air conditioning because it felt similar to the heat outside the building. During summer, Townsville can experience anywhere between thirty-two and forty-five degrees. Wearing a woolly knitted jumper in the middle of summer in Townsville was suicidal at best. Going from sixteen and eighteen degrees into that temperature and back again wreaked havoc on my sinuses. I suffered cold after flu after cold, coupled with four massive nose bleeds. I used all my sick days within a month.

Yet this was only the tip of the iceberg. Looking back, I suffered various symptoms, from wanting to fall asleep at my desk, to loss of situational awareness, to shivering, to loss of ability to speak properly, to being unable to handle basic objects like pens or phones, to breathing difficulties and a few other symptoms that had all the hallmarks of hypothermia. On top of this, my productivity was falling.

When I complained to management about the situation, even giving them a solution to bring the back workers to the front and I would work in the back, they did bugger all. Nothing was done and I knew they had failed their WHS policies. But that wasn't what forced me out of the office.

All my time working there I would go out of my way to help people. If they asked for help, I would always say yes. Yet, after the air conditioning event, when I asked a colleague to help me, she flat out said, 'Fuck off. I have my own work.' And yes, she was one I helped a lot.

We all have moments of intense rage and want to flay people alive, but usually these thoughts come in the heat of the moment and quickly fade. The one I developed, to strangle the blood out of the bitch, held fast for three days straight. The following week I dreaded even walking through the office door. I simply didn't wish to return because I feared I would end up killing someone — and I wasn't the target.

For once doctors actually helped me. They gave me the motivation I needed to find another job, but I chose it out of desperation to get away from a toxic environment. It was school portrait photography with very bad equipment. The team was fantastic, no bullying or harassment, but because of the poor un-ergonomic tools of the trade, I ended up with Achilles tendonitis, which rendered me out of commission within the first year.

I ended up as a receptionist at a physio with only fifteen hours a week work, which suited me fine until the owner sold the business and the new boss reduced my hours to eight a week. I couldn't live on that. Finances were the driving force in helping me find another job. My mistake was that I scored a traineeship which only lasted eighteen weeks before 2019 arrived with no work in sight.

The torture didn't stop. Unemployment is mentally challenging. Its language is silence, one that drills dread into your soul and allows bad thoughts to flourish. You begin thinking, 'what is wrong with me?' and, 'I'm worthless. I must be if no one is bothering to respond to my applications', followed with, 'why should I get out of bed today?' or better yet, 'why should I continue living?'

Unemployment steals all sense of humanity from you. You are not part of the working world, nor part of society. You cannot be human in that case. They show no interest in you, therefore you can be nothing but an alien. If I was the alien, where the hell did I park my spaceship? More importantly, where did I put the keys?

You lose all sense of motivation and interest. I gained weight which added to the torture. I couldn't exercise because I simply couldn't care. I was worthless. I wasn't even human. Why was I living in the first place?

I eventually found a job as a school crossing guard supervisor. The only problem with this job was the drivers. The team was fabulous, the kids friendly. But the drivers? Have no intelligence whatsoever.

When you see a big red STOP sign in the middle of the road, you are meant to remove your foot from the accelerator and apply it gently to the brakes to bring your vehicle to a halt, allowing the guard to cross people from one side of the road to the other safely. I feel some drivers see it backwards and think we are dope-smoking idiots who don't know what we're doing, reading it as POTS. You know, doing pot? MJ? Smoking weed?

One who stands out pretty much sums up all the aggressive drivers on the road. Because it says, 'Children's Crossing', people think only kids are allowed to cross over. They forget there are teachers and parents. They further forget there are people who need to cross to get to a bus stop. It is a public domain. Ergo anyone can use it. And the crossing guards are a free service, why not use them?

Some drivers get upset when you stop them, even if you are packing up after your shift. One car was far down the road, we would have crossed easily without stopping it had the driver not been speeding. By the time the car reached us we were almost off the second carriage — his carriage.

Instead of speeding away, he waited for us to be together — the other lady had to collect her flag — and edged forward with his window down. He yelled out, 'Next time fucking wait for traffic to pass before crossing out. There are no fucking kids around.' He sped off. This is the lamest form of abuse crossing guards receive. Many get it right in their faces. Some are physically hit. And if they are elderly, like some guards are, the police get involved allowing more stress to enter their lives.

Even in the working world, I received abuse from all sides. Customers, drivers, colleagues — hell, even the equipment wasn't kind to me. There was no escape. The more abuse I received, the less I wanted to be around people. How could I trust them? My paranoia was telling me, 'Why bother trying to find a friend. They're only going to treat you the same way.'

Why did I think this? Because everyone I met treated me poorly in one way or another. By the time I found my last job — warehouse work — I expected the same treatment. However, I have found hope.

Ninety per cent of the workforce at the factory are male. I

feel like I'm in a jungle of men. And some of their language would make a feminist explode. Thank God I'm not one of them. It's all in jest, it's all fun, it's not directed at anyone to insult or cause harm. It is very entertaining letting men be themselves. And above all, they treat me with respect. They are all kind, wonderful people, who quickly made me feel like I have found a home away from home. They joke, they laugh, and yes, there are pranks. But instead of telling them off or feeling like I have been made a fool, they show it is all in jest and not to be taken seriously. And even I'm starting to act like them, even telling some, in a joking manner, to 'fuck off'. (*Give me a break, okay. He wanted me to clean his dishes.*)

I have warmed up to them and can let my hair down — relatively speaking. (*You can't wear your hair out in a bread factory. It's tied up in a bun and under a hairnet. Doubt anyone would want to pull a foot long hair out of a loaf of bread.*) The environment is friendly, open, and above all, humane. And yes, I have been pranked by the big boss, telling me my manager wanted to see me only to find out he didn't. And in the immortal words of our fun safety officer, 'It is okay to have fun.'

Back to my earlier chapter, *Lack of Engagement*, I am starting to engage with the guys at the factory more often. I don't have to wait for them to engage first; I initiate it. It's amazing how being treated with respect can bring out the human in you, allowing you to ditch the alien effect once and for all.

I think sometimes, 'Why the hell didn't I join factory work in the first place? Why did I have to suffer all that abuse from all corners of society? What was the point of it all?'

Well, the point was, no matter where you go, you're going to find people who simply don't care how badly they treat you. Some people are jerks and arseholes and although you can't control their behaviour, you can control your own. You have one of two choices:

1. You can become as nasty as them and sell out your integrity, or
2. You can ignore them and find something better to go to, leaving them in the dirt they call home.

In the end, I chose the latter. I will not sell out my integrity. I am better than them. I have the strength and resilience to avoid suicidal thoughts and learnt my lesson that I will never let anyone ever get the better of me again.

But despite learning this lesson, my experiences still drive my distrust issues. Opening up to people is difficult because at the back of my mind, there is this little paranoid voice saying, 'They will betray you.' It is why I find myself in corners at parties or don't go to parties at all.

As for my warehouse colleagues, I can joke with them, talk to them, and not fear any reprisals. But it took three months to get to that point. They did try to invite me out to drinks at the beginning, twice, but I had other things on at the time. There was a third invite, but unfortunately, we never exchanged numbers. One got sick and the other forgot, and there I was, at the pub, looking for them. The first time I forced myself out of the house to 'engage' and I got stood up. (*Sorry for pointing this out guys.*) But I don't blame them; no numbers were exchanged to let me know. It was a lesson learnt. Next time we'll have those numbers ready. And in the theme of having fun, we laughed it off.

CHAPTER 15

I was a romantic, dammit!

I've never celebrated a first anniversary with anyone, ever. I always had plans to celebrate it with the one I loved. I never got the chance. I had several ideas, but only one stuck. It taunts me these days as if telling me, 'You'll never get to do this, ever.' (*Nice to know my thoughts bully me too*). And it might be too 1950s, but it's not like I would do this every single day. These types of things have magic if done once in a while; that magic wears off if it's expected every day.

I had a lot to give. Perhaps I gave it all away. No. I have potential, but I have placed it in a box, packed it up and shoved it in a dungeon in my mind, locking the gate and having the key lost to the sands of time.

I desired desperately to share it, to let my partner know how much I loved him (*I know I had lesbian experiences, but given I switched off, I'll use the male term)*. I might not be able to experience it, ever, but I would like to at least let someone know what I would have done. This might be overkill, but it highlights how much I would have done for my beloved. It could have been a waste of time nor had the effect I desired. I'll never know. But if I had to celebrate a first anniversary, this is what I would have done.

I would assume to be living with my partner by this time. If not, I would arrange to sleep over the day before. I would wake silently and go to the kitchen to prepare breakfast. I would return to the bedroom and softly wake my lover with gentle words, caressing strokes over the forehead or down the cheek, perhaps a kiss, and bid him a good morning with breakfast in bed.

As he eats, I would sit beside him and talk, find out how he slept, if he dreamt anything, how he felt and what he thought the day had in store for him. When he finished, I would take the tray and tell him to go freshen up. While he did, I would make the bed and lay out whatever clothes he would normally wear — uniform or casual — before heading back to the kitchen to start cleaning.

If he had to leave for work, I would ensure his things were ready. This would include a paper bag with a prepared lunch and a little love note with a kind word or two inside, declaring my love. I would walk him to the car, giving him a kiss goodbye. While he was at work, I would go out and buy a bottle of good red wine and a dozen roses. By this time, I would know what his favourite item would be, or what he wanted in a gift, and have it ready for him too.

Before he returned home, I would scatter the petals of six roses on the bed. The other half dozen I would place all but one in a vase with a bow and a card holding sweet words, telling him how much I appreciate him, how he makes me feel and promising to bring him happiness and joy as best as I could.

I would cook him his favourite meal and prepare a candlelight dinner table. I would have soft music playing — I like Billie Holiday's *The Very Thought of You* — and when he arrives home, I would greet him at the door with a glass of wine and single red rose, meeting him with a kiss.

There is probably a lot more I would do after this point, but I'm making myself depressed. There is no point fantasising about something that can never happen. But you can see I have potential. And with this, perhaps love hasn't left me after all. It's locked away somewhere, waiting for the one person who finds the key and frees it from the prison, allowing it to rear its ugly head once more. *(Might be Shrek for all I know.)*

All my lovers never got to see this potential. I guess they can see what they are missing. And as for the next one that comes along, it will all depend on how he treats me before I ever consider giving too much of my heart and soul away again.

CHAPTER 16

StarKnight and Sunshine

Around mid-2021, when the loneliness really started to bite and the world looked to be facing an ever-growing pandemic without end, I guess I had a midlife crisis. I envy those in my position because many seem to be able to afford sports cars or rare motorbikes or some expensive daredevil stunt or enjoy a holiday. Me? I wasn't able to do such crazy spending. My low wage-earning job wouldn't allow it. And considering I was on the bare minimum wage for six years, there was no way I was going to afford my hobbies and buy something I can ill afford at the same time. Instead, I wrote a book.

Yes, two dreams started me on this past-trekking path, but one specific day sparked my midlife crisis. I wanted simply to talk to someone only to find there was no one there, not even my mother because she was out doing the grocery shopping. I discovered myself in a dilemma; if she passed away, who would be there for me? I have a sister who has no time on her hands to spare for me; my uncles and aunts live in Sydney and I am too far away to visit, not that we could travel at the time as the border was closed and they had their own problems to deal with, why would I add to them? I have cousins but had not seen any in more than ten years; I was practically non-existent to them. And I have my dog, but she was getting on in years and it wouldn't be too long before she too left me.

I could always get another dog, but what I discovered was I needed human companionship. Someone to talk to and engage with socially, enjoy a coffee or a stiff drink, or perhaps walk along the beach or play tennis. However, it had been five years since my last social meeting, not counting theatre productions, but no one talked much with me at those events either. I had no friends.

I didn't know where to begin, but I knew the first step would be simply to do something. And the first thing I had to do was fight my distrust issues, quickly followed with a forceful attitude to push myself and reach out.

Using the only social platform I had active at the time, which I hardly used, I connected to a few people I knew from the theatre. I thought they would be the best place to start because they knew me, or at least semi-knew me. While they accepted the connections, they also said, 'Don't use this site much, you probably won't hear from me here.' Naturally, no other contact details were specified. The social connections were marred from the start. What good is a connection if they don't communicate?

But one person stood out. And this guy is the bravest of them all. He is the one who allowed me to use his name without alteration. Despite his approval, I had an alias set up in case he said no, and I want to keep it because it is him to a tee. Cupid. The little cherub of love. (*Although with his height, he is anything but a cherub*). And he did bring love back into my life.

Cupid and I acted in a couple of plays. When I first met him, he came across as an over-sexed maniac (*sorry sweetie*). Let me explain: when he introduced himself, I stretched out my hand, as was the custom when handshakes were the norm, and he grabbed mine. It wasn't hard or strong, but his index finger tickled my palm incessantly. This immediately brought a flashback conversation I had with my mother years ago: 'If a man ever tickles your palm when you shake his hand, it means he wants sex with you.'

Ah, the weird old ways of courting. I thought she was joking but Cupid proved otherwise. It was enough to alert me to his intentions and I stayed the hell away from him. It didn't offend me; it didn't insult me. I guess I was flattered to know that was what he wanted — he would have been the first one wanting it from me in twenty years. But, at the time, I was in a place of keeping to myself, distrusting everyone and not wanting that complexity in my life. It was far better for me to avoid him than encourage him. I didn't ignore him though; I would greet him, but that's as far as the conversation would go.

During the second play in 2018, I could see he had some problems. He didn't come across as his usual self. I tried to engage, but he was distant. Given we weren't anything other than castmates, I didn't take it personally and gave him the space he needed. Besides, I was in no mental state to engage with anyone.

One of the first things he sent me after I requested a connection, was an apology.

'I am sorry if my past behaviour caused you any distress and/or was insulting or offensive.'

That was the start of his rather long email. I replied saying, 'You never offended me, never insulted me, or caused distress. I found you a bit strong in behaviour, but definitely not offensive.'

And with that, he kept emailing me. We kept conversing, understanding each other, learning. He had problems. We all do. I didn't know how deep those problems were until much later. And I wasn't going to say, 'Sorry, can't do this friendship because you have problems.' That was not right. And I was only looking for a friend. But had I known where it would lead, I should have pulled out all stops from the start, if anything to not cause him any more pain.

To say Cupid was a mistake would be the worst fake news revelation in history. He certainly was nothing of the sort;

he was an experience.

Our connection started on 25 September 2021. Two weeks later, on 8 October, we kissed. But I'm getting ahead of myself. In those two weeks, we learnt a little of our likes, not many dislikes though, which I think would have been a great source of information for me to decide if I really wanted to get involved with him. He made me feel something I hadn't felt since 2017, the year when Verdandi destroyed all emotion in me.

Love is a strange concept, an alien force. It reaches into your heart and soul and makes you feel ecstatic things you would never feel otherwise. It also knocks senses out of orbit, and they take a little while to come back into the fold and make you see things clearly.

What started it all was *Ghostbusters*. Yes, *Ghostbusters*.

Let me build you some context.

One of my hobbies is building large Lego sets and putting lights in them. It is a very time-consuming pastime, especially when some sets have 8,000 pieces. I tried doing both at the same time and got confused because the lighting instructions start with disassembling the object from the end to the beginning, but building is from beginning to end. I build the sets first and install the lights last. Can take weeks.

One of the things I built and lighted was the *Ghostbusters* Ecto-1 vehicle. I took photos and a video of it, sharing them with Cupid. He responded with a photo of him dressed as Spangler, complete with proton pack and the little spectrometer gizmo. I couldn't help but respond with, 'in the immortal words of Doctor Venkman, 'nice shootin' Tex'.'

And from that point, we were sharing *Ghostbusters* quotes like a badly timed tennis match. Three hours of it. (*Don't look at me like that!*) Everyone has their quirks. It intensified the friendship like a rocket had fired, going from zero to a thousand in less than a second. Okay, overstating it here, but you get the general idea.

After realising we could spend all day wasting time, I told him as much, saying, 'Next thing you'll be throwing *Star Wars* quotes.'

This did not discourage him. He simply responded with, 'Describe your sex life using *Star Wars* quotes: "You came in that thing? You're braver than I thought".'

Really, that's what he chose to do. Sexuality based on *Star Wars* quotes. Princess Leia in the gold bikini. Need I say more? (*RIP Carrie Fisher.*) But we enjoyed a little tit-for-tat with those quotes as well. I guess when you're bored out of your mind the simplest things can entertain.

I wasn't looking for love, but somehow love found me. His problems didn't even fathom into my decision. Why should they? As I said, we all have problems. Even a recruiter told me, 'People our age are not going to be pristine. I'm living proof.'

It was on that world-shattering night, 8 October, when we dined at a restaurant. It was a pleasant-enough evening, the meal was fantastic, the restaurant noise could have been less, but find me a quiet dining place in Australia other than home. Take what you can get. As we were leaving, I went to hug him goodbye. He lent down and kissed me on the lips.

Time stood still. I swear I saw the DeLorean's fire trail pass by a couple of times. Two things happened, hitting me at eighty-eight miles an hour. First, a little voice appeared in my head asking me, 'What is this weird thing stuck to your lips?' and 'What the fuck is going on?' I gathered this came from the part of me that shrieks in terror at the sight of a spider or cowers under the bedsheets when lightning strikes.

The other thing that happened was a blood rush. It had been twenty years since someone had kissed me on the lips. Blood rushed to my head. I felt like fainting. I actually pulled away from him to steady myself and think. Could I think? Was I thinking? No, I wasn't. He had kissed all thoughts out of me. But I saw his expression as if he had done the worst thing in the world and lost my respect.

When the blood rush stopped, the thoughts flowed. Cower Girl started snapping at me. 'Don't stop you fool!' (*Seriously, can't make her out sometimes.*) But I followed her instruction. I reached up to his head and pulled him down for another kiss. And with that, our relationship was sealed.

Our flirting intensified. Feelings were uncontrollable. And one night — before my birthday — I was in the throes of ecstasy as he brought me to an orgasmic explosion. The first anyone has given me in twenty years.

However — yes, there is a however in this part of the story — we never shared penetrative sex. Not to say we didn't try, we did, but it brought about a new revelation in the story that is my life.

The night he tried; we had been fooling around for a while. After a slight penetration, he slipped out but didn't try again. Think we were simply tired. When we started to compose ourselves, he looked down at himself and saw blood. It was mine. What do you expect after twenty years? Even machines seize up if they haven't been used for a long time.

It was all consenting. He didn't hurt me. It was not painful. It was a shock. Cupid was gentle in all aspects of the lovemaking. He was giving — oh so giving — and attentive. The problem we discovered, well the doctor did after I visited her after a two-year hiatus, was I suffer from post-coital bleeding. This is a condition where women bleed during sex. I had to be referred to a gynaecologist. What she found was everything was okay, hunky-dory, nothing out of the ordinary in the biopsy and that was it. (*The bleeding was what? Paint?*) She wanted me to continue 'trying' sex to see if it repeated. Never in my life had any of my prescriptions been, 'have more sex'.

Unfortunately — yes there is one of those here too — I never got the opportunity. Let me explain why.

When we discovered the blood, I was kind of scared to do it again. Cupid's expression was of such remorse and horror, I didn't want to see that again. I felt it caused him a lot of pain and I didn't want to add to his problems. Conceivably, lack of sex could cause harm too. Not only was I scared of hurting

Cupid but I was more scared of being hurt myself. Bleeding during sex is not normal.

The other thing stopping me from engaging in coitus exposed itself on 1 January 2022. (*Great start to the year.*) This one is also another condition women will experience. Prepare yourself ladies.

It started in my chest, or more accurately on my chest. My breasts felt weird — can't really describe it other than weird — they felt heavy as if someone had strapped ten-ton weights to them. I couldn't rub them either because they were extremely tender; a thousand papercuts would have been a nicer experience. They were exceedingly sensitive that doing anything that involved a slight bumping motion — like walking — was painful, similar to being kicked in the groin. I found I had to cradle both breasts as I walked and tread slowly without too much bouncing motion. Awkward and frustrating. On top of this, taking deep breaths felt like someone was digging knives into my lungs, affecting my breathing and causing me to feel extra tired because my body wasn't getting the required oxygen to function. Back to the doctor I went and, luckily, was able to get an ultrasound the next day rather than the two weeks wait it would have been if a cancellation hadn't occurred. And they found a problem. (*Yes, another one. It doesn't pay to be a woman.*)

Do you know the diameter of a golf ball? It's 42.7 mm. I have a cyst in my right breast that is 44 mm. That's right, it's bigger than a golf ball. The diagnosis was fibrocystic disease, but it isn't a disease because it isn't inherited nor is it contagious. It's a hormonal thing. Sixty per cent of women will experience it when they go through the dreaded change. My aunt said she had one in the 1970s and her doctor put her on a three-month course of antibiotics. It dried up and cleared the problem.

I was offered no treatment other than to take a non-medically-approved solution of primrose oil tablets to dull the pain. If it became unbearable, which it was at the time but subsided when I next spoke to the doctor about the results, they could drain it. This means getting another ultrasound referral, waiting for God knows how long and suffering the excruciating pain it caused. A syringe is plunged into the breast from the other side to where the cyst resides to draw out the contents, slowly, with no anaesthetic — unless I misunderstood. And as for antibiotics? They no longer give these out unless the cyst is infected.

I saw three doctors and none offered any help, not even wanting to touch it because it's in the breast and there are important glands there you need apparently. Some doctors won't see me because I'm not privately insured (*talk about discrimination. Does that belong to a Hippocratic oath?*) There are those doctors who don't want to take on any more patients. And lastly, the breast screening clinic couldn't help me because the cyst has become noticeable; they only look for symptoms before they appear.

What I know about cysts is this: if you don't remove the

sac, they grow back. How often will I need to return to the clinic — at $118 a visit — to get the darn thing drained? I don't trust doctors as much as I don't trust people. That is why I had a hiatus of seeing them for two years. This distrust comes from the fact that all my life I have had one of these two diagnoses: 'There is nothing wrong with you' or 'It's all in your head'. (*If the problem is in my head, why do I have a lump in my breast?*)

The reason for these two diagnoses is simply due to delayed testing. When you see a doctor, if you can see them on the day of the problem — most times you must wait two to three weeks and the problem disappears by the time you visit — he or she refers you to get tested. But you must also wait to get tested. In my cases, when I needed testing the waiting period allowed the problem to sort itself out. By the time the examinations were undertaken there was nothing to be found, thus there was nothing wrong with me, by their reckoning. The symptoms returned many times.

Lumbered with these two problems I was scared to get naked with Cupid again. Plus, I wanted to wait for the specialist's report before I re-engaged in sex, and I had to wait until March for that visit. For three months we both suffered a lack of sex. Cruel really, after twenty years I get a glimmer of hope only to see it snatched away because of physical problems and fear of making them worse.

My relationship with Cupid was an eye opener for me. He claimed he didn't know how to love someone, and I found I had to guide him on a few aspects to which my Cower Girl started screaming at me, 'You shouldn't have to do this, he is old enough to know better,' followed with, 'Why are you guiding this guy on how to show you love and affection? It's like you're trying to date yourself.' At least with my other relationships I didn't have to tell them anything other than aspects of my life.

I'll give you an example:

One dinner date, we went to a restaurant. He opened the door and, as some stranger was stepping out, he stepped aside and held the door open for the man. I could see he had courtesy in his blood. But after the stranger departed Cupid stepped in and let go of the door. Had I not held my arm out to stop it, I would have got a face full of glass and metal. I had to call him on it, telling him it hurt that he held it open for a stranger but not his girlfriend. Afterwards he opened doors for me. Was I expecting too much? No. I've read stories of women who complain about men not doing this on their dates. I'm not alone.

I honestly feel sorry for men these days because there are many women out there who take offence to courteous things like holding a door open for them. I know this is fact because one day I saw a woman struggling with some shopping bags as she was approaching a door. I held the door open for her. She didn't look at me, she glared and snapped, 'What do you think I am, an invalid?' They exist. Because of these types of women men are scared to do what should come naturally.

They are either damned if they do, or damned if they don't. They can't win.

Claiming he didn't know how to love someone should have been a massive red flag, but silly me ignored it. (*Love and blindness go hand in hand.*) I didn't know how to love someone either. It had been years since I was in a relationship. Yet the skills are there, slightly rusty but available if I look hard enough. But I had to guide him. I have never had to tell people anything like this before, it made me feel all wrong. It made me feel I was moulding him into what I wanted out of a partner without any input from him, thus he would become something he wasn't meant to become. That meant I would be manipulating him despite trying to help him. In other words, it made me feel like I was forcing my opinions and faith onto him. And like I said before, how can you respect someone who does that? It made me feel bad.

Yet he did something that disproved his claim. He was enraptured, calling me Sunshine, 'Because you bring sunshine into my dark life.' That touched me. None of my other partners gave me nicknames. Wait, I think Larunda called me Bubbles only because I told her my joints pop and snap. You know, 'snap crackle and pop' Rice Bubbles.

Further to his nickname for me, one of the gifts he got me was a little music box which played *You Are My Sunshine*. How can this not be love? How can he claim he doesn't know how to love when this clearly shows he does?

And given he gave me a nickname, I thought it fitting to

find one for him. He suggested a couple that seemed lame in comparison. 'Captain Underpants Jelly Crystals' didn't seem appropriate, especially after the books were banned for racist and violent content. Apparently, it was a children's series, something he liked when he was a kid.

StarKnight came about because he said his life was dark. Stars are at their best when it is night, shining for all the world to see. He certainly became a star in my life at that point in time. And 'knight' is a twist of night = dark and knight = saviour. How he made me feel proved he was a knight in shining armour. Knights are the embodiment of all things good — or at least that is what we have been led to believe. He also proved that my decision to fight my distrust issues was the correct move because now I could move forward with someone.

StarKnight and Sunshine, sitting in a tree ...

We agreed communication was key to a good relationship. But I found he couldn't be serious. He was always joking or quoting comedians or shifting the focus of the conversation away from what should have been a serious topic. I agree laughter is a great bonding technique, but it should be kept to a minimum. A relationship cannot be built on comedy alone. And when he was serious, it was only to discuss his problems. I know relationships are for better or for worse, but it shouldn't be stuck on a single topic.

I had to tell him he was unloading on me too much, I couldn't cope. I wanted to help but didn't know how, and

I felt overburdened. He agreed. And that's when I noticed he tended to agree with me a lot. I don't think he actually thought the issues through, instead agreeing in the hope I wouldn't leave him. Possibly this was my paranoia at work again. I didn't break up with him. I could have easily done this but I didn't because I felt we could move forward without him encumbering me with his problems.

But as with a lot of relationships, the more you learn, the more you feel like you've made a big mistake. As I said before, Cupid was not; he was an experience.

I think I had to come into his life to give him the courage to do what he needed to in order to set him on the path to recovery. He said I gave him courage and confidence to find a job. He believed it would speed his recovery.

He taught me the art of relationships and what I needed to vet in order to find the right person for me. In some ways, Cupid was the right person; in others, not so much. As with all relationships, the experience teaches you what you need to learn.

One of the first things we agreed on was communication. Relationships are doomed to fail without it. And one of the things he understood was the reward gained by confronting problems early; that when they are communicated it is often too late by the time they become problematic and instead of talking, you're yelling and being abusive. We didn't want that. However, my pacifist and non-confrontational nature prevented me from airing problems when they arose. I would later write him an email about the issue and wait for his reply, which either came in a short email or SMS text. That was something I had to work on; I still do.

I noticed another problem on my birthday. This was the first birthday in two years I truly enjoyed. Before cooking me a nice fish and chips meal, he spoilt me with multiple gifts and poems he wrote. He is a talented poet. His work is sublime. A Wordsworth-worthy effort. This wasn't the problem. It happened when we sat down to eat ...

When I'm at home with mum, we sit at the table for dinner and talk. There is no other distraction. We have been doing this for years. It was what I expected. You go to restaurants and people are eating and talking. That's why it's noisy. It appears to be the norm. But at Cupid's place? He sat and glued his eyes to the television off my left shoulder. He was so enthralled with what was showing on the box that he didn't hear my question, even after I repeated it. To this day, I can't remember what that question was, because over the years I have trained and programmed myself that if someone doesn't respond or engage with me after the second attempt, I give up and don't bother, and quickly forget what I wanted to know.

That was the first time I noticed it. It happened again a few weeks after Christmas when the movie *Twister* was playing. He can quote that movie word for word, line for line. Again, he was more interested in quoting a movie than engaging with me while he ate dinner.

I noticed the problem again. This time, with cricket. I

know men and their fanatical ways with sport. Hell, some women are enthusiasts as well. He had it playing in the car ride to the restaurant on one date and when we got to our table, he sat in a position where he could see the game on the television behind me. I tried engaging with him, but he seemed distant. I don't think that was entirely due to the game; he had found a new job and was called in a lot during the week leading up to our date. He looked very tired.

I told him, 'If you're tired, we can do this another time.' He said he didn't want to because he felt guilty not spending enough time with me. And at dinner, he was distant and distracted, he didn't communicate much, if at all. Quite frankly, I didn't know what to make of it other than it was a problem I could see manifesting into a nuclear scenario. As he wasn't engaging on the date, I decided it would be pointless to argue the point because he wasn't going to listen anyway. I should have aired it right there.

I think the reason I delayed airing the problem was simply this: Cupid was the first person I had engaged with socially in about five years. He was the first person to engage with me, without strings attached, without force, without reason. I had only found him. I thought if I aired the problems, I'd lose him.

After a twenty-year sexual dry spell, love found me. I wanted to please him because of the way he made me feel. I wanted it because I had been denied it for years. And here I was, starting my menopause, trying to achieve the impossible.

The cysts in the breasts made it impossible to walk, let alone have sex, and the post-coital bleeding made both of us uncomfortable. It seemed our relationship was plagued with problems, but I still wanted it.

Why did I feel airing problems felt like I would lose everything? Ask my paranoia, that little devil mental creep born by all the bullying and bad treatment I had over the years. It still dictates how I approach problems. My pacifist ways and not wanting to engage in confrontation hindered any attempt to fix this problem when it happened. This showed me I must be stronger. I wish I was because this inattention problem manifested into something worse: ignoring me.

He loves his football. He has a favourite team. And when they lose, he sulks. I guess every fan has his day and his quirks. But when a football team loses and I don't hear a response from him when I send a text or email until after twenty-four hours. Why? Why should I have to suffer silence because a football team lost? I found this unfair. It was a deafening silence that ate at my soul, shredded my patience and made me question the entire relationship.

Cupid is the sweetest person I have met. I have nothing bad to say about him other than his silences. His television distractions at dinner could be fixed, but his ignoring me was going to take a lot of time and place a heavy toll on me. I had suffered enough in my life; I didn't want to suffer more. Yes, I made the mistake of going in for that second kiss and igniting this relationship without full knowledge of what I was getting into. I take full responsibility for that. But I was desperate. Common sense didn't factor into my decision; it didn't even exist.

To me, a romantic relationship is a prelude to marriage. And marriage is for better or for worse. But we were not married. If this was how he behaved when we were dating, I could expect worse when we were married. I couldn't see myself marrying someone who, when he was upset because a football team lost, would ignore me. How can anyone justify that?

I emailed him and told him his silence was hurting me. I told him he needed to make a decision on where we go from here, not have me do it for him because his opinions counted.

He texted me saying he wanted to talk about it. It was Good Friday 14 April 2022 — not a really good day in the end. After a short day's work, I called him.

'You wanted to talk about my email,' I said, with a little dread in my heart.

'Do you want me to do this by email, text or face to face?'

I chose face to face. I needed to see him. I think it was inevitable what he was going to do and it wouldn't be right to do it in an email or over the phone.

Honestly, I didn't want to break up with him. I was trying to help. I didn't want to make all the decisions in the relationship. His input mattered too but he was — gutless is not the word. Scared to commit. Possibly fearing he would lose me by making a decision I might not like. If I didn't like it, we could have negotiated. I was blindly hoping he would use some of my words to strengthen his resolve, take a risk and make a decision.

It was not to be. Our relationship ended. He believed he took on too much at once and needed to step back. Out of respect for his situation, I had to agree.

The relationship was not a mistake. It was an experience. It showed me I am still capable of loving someone. Cupid gave me that at least. And I hope I did bring a little sunshine to his life, to prove it is still out there for him.

I think the lesson I learnt is not to rush into anything, desperation needs to be ignored for the sake of mental sanity. I need to test prospective partners more before involving myself deeper with them. An ill-informed decision cannot lead to a good future. An emotion-fuelled decision usually leads to disaster.

We have brains. We think. Therefore, we are. And if we do not think before we act, we must learn from the lesson. Otherwise, what's the point of owning a brain?

And given Cupid was nine and a half years my junior — yes, for about six months I was a cougar (*meow*) — I guess my mother's advice wasn't as bad as I imagined. However, it wasn't our age that broke us up.

EPILOGUE

What happens next?

There you have it. The story of my sex and social life. Don't feel sorry for me, that's not what I'm aiming for, but if you do, thank you for the thought. My life highlights how bullying can affect a person, not only at school but throughout life. And Australia is rife with bullies.

It's amazing how a simple flash of a celebrity's face in a dream could conjure up a story like this. Reminiscing about my past has been a fun trip and a revelation. I have the ability to love and be loved; the challenge is in not only finding it but also keeping it alive. If I can make it past a first anniversary, then I have learnt the trick.

Dredging up the past doesn't have to be terrible. It opens your eyes. Helps you understand. Teaches you the mistakes you have made to help avoid repeats in the future, or you can use those mistakes to push yourself forward faster — like my mind did with the English actor. It is your history. It is what makes you, you. It doesn't have to hold you back and, yes, letting go can help you move forward, but some things should never be forgotten.

Not everyone has a good life. I'm one of them. Some people hate their past to extremes that they hide it — which is what I think Larunda did. Either that, or she was scared of herself, not wanting to face old wounds and deal with them. But you cannot fight your fears by running from them. Easier said than done and a lesson I should use for my other problems. One day I will; at least Cupid proved I can do it.

Some of the experiences I've shared are shameful — like when I was ten. I do feel ashamed of that, but I was a kid. How was I supposed to know? I am not ashamed of what I am, who I am, or my life choices. I don't hate anyone from my past. I despise the bullies and those lovers who took advantage or made me sick, or friends who couldn't accept no for an answer. But never hate. Hate is a powerful word I don't like using. As for those who failed to impress, they were mere bumps in the journey that is my life. A lesson learnt.

Do I have any regrets? I could say I regret writing this, but I don't. Even though someone might come along and make me choke on these words. As for my life, the only thing I do regret are my suicide attempts. To allow a bunch of girls to get the better of me is regretful. The lesson being, to never let it happen again.

And while I don't regret the failed romances — they obviously weren't for me — I only wish I'd found the one. I am still capable of loving. But you can't cry over spilt milk, you must clean it up and learn to pour the milk a different way.

Who knows? A new regret might emerge, because I am wondering what happens if any of these people read my book and come back into my life? Interesting question. I might sit for a coffee and reminisce, but I most likely wouldn't get back together with them. What they did was too painful. Yet I can't see any of them doing this; I think they would prefer to forget me.

As for the handsome artist fantasy that started all this, I have no idea what I would do if I met him. I don't know what he would do. I think I would be too embarrassed to meet and possibly ashamed. I wouldn't even be able to look him in the eyes. Pity, they were the best part of him — I loved his gorgeous eyes.

If I have one lesson to pass on, it would be to think before you act. Don't rush into things. Don't be quick to give things away, especially your virginity. Once it has been given, you can't get it back, despite what Chandler Bing said. Learn to trust the person before you commit. It might save you from a world of pain.

Thank you for joining me on this journey. It has been therapeutic. Thank you for investing time in my life. I'm happy I could share something with you. At least I know when I pass on, someone somewhere will know a little piece of me.

And last but not least, one thing I can say for certain — thanks to the guys at work — is, "It is okay to have fun." As long as it doesn't hurt anyone.

www.ingramcontent.com/pod-product-compliance
Lightning Source LLC
Chambersburg PA
CBHW030256010526
44107CB00053B/1740